THE SERIOUS JAZZ BOOK II
THE HARMONIC APPROACH

(Harmonic Possibilities of the Improvised Line)

by Barry Finnerty

Editor and Publisher - Chuck Sher
Graphics & Cover design - Attila Nagy
Cover Art - fractal by Cory Ench
www.enchgallery.com

TABLE OF CONTENTS

About The Author

Barry Finnerty is a guitar legend, having played and recorded with many of the best musicians in jazz and fusion—including Airto & Flora Purim, Chico Hamilton, Hubert Laws, Joe Farrell, Ray Barretto, Blood Sweat & Tears, Taj Mahal, Billy Cobham and the Thad Jones/Mel Lewis band.

Barry was the guitarist on several seminal recordings in the 1970s and 1980s, including Miles Davis' "The Man With The Horn", the Brecker Brothers' "Heavy Metal Bebop", and the Crusaders' "Street Life".

Born in the San Francisco Bay Area, Barry moved to New York in 1973, played with the above-mentioned artists (and many more), toured with the Crusaders for four years, and then moved back to the Bay Area in 1998, where he currently plays, teaches, composes and records. His latest records are available at www.barryfinnerty.com. He can be reached at barry@barryfinnerty.com.

Barry is also the author of the widely-acclaimed *The Serious Jazz Practice Book*, available from Sher Music Co., www.shermusic.com, or at better music stores worldwide.

Special Thanks

To Chuck and Attila at Sher Music, to Randy Vincent and Ruth Finnerty for their dedicated and meticulous proofreading, to the people at Sibelius for their great tech support, to B.B. King, Mike Brecker, Randy Brecker, Dave Kikoski, Victor Bailey, Ron McClure, Chuggy Carter, Graham Hawthorne, Victor Jones, Hubert Laws, Joe Lovano, Mark Levine, all the people that bought *The Serious Jazz Practice Book* and all the people that buy this one! And also of course to my love, Clarita.

Dedication

For Jim Checkley, wherever you are... thanks for the idea!

INTRODUCTION

The original title of this book was: "Harmonic Possibilities of the Improvised Line". An intriguing concept. Does an improvised line, i.e. a jazz solo, actually *have* harmonic possibilities? And if so, what are they? Isn't it enough to know the correct scales to go with the chords in whatever song you are playing, and then just let your creativity take over? Or can a melody being spontaneously improvised over chord changes actually go one step further than that? Can the modern jazz soloist create melodies that really reflect and embody the harmonies of the chords in the tune he is improvising over? Can he develop his melodies based on extended *harmonic* creativity, chord substitutions, etc? Is it possible for the player to really *get inside* the harmony of a tune and achieve real harmonic *and* melodic control of *every note he is playing?*

Well, yes. It can be done. And this book is being written to light the way.

In my last book, *The Serious Jazz Practice Book,* I tried to put forth a guide to getting just about every possible combination of *melodic* materials under the fingers of the modern jazz soloist. To give the player a vast and varied musical vocabulary to be used for the creation of *melody.*

But *harmony* is different from melody. The harmony of a tune is part of its structure and foundation. Harmony happens, chords change, over time, at specific points in time, and the modern jazz soloist must be aware of those points and be sure to adjust his spontaneity, his creativity, his improvisation accordingly. There are so many ways to do this, and variations upon variations, but with dedication and study I believe that it can be mastered. (To get started with this book, you should have at least a basic knowledge of scales, modes, and chord formation.)

A very important thing to remember, in my opinion, is that playing and improvising over chord changes is first of all an exercise in *correctness.* The *craft* of it comes first; the *art* comes later. If the soloist is not fully conscious of the prevailing harmony and (at least) the correct notes that can (and should!) be played against it, the music will definitely suffer. I think musicians should have to take kind of a jazz version of the Hippocratic Oath like doctors are required to do before they are allowed to practice: "First, do no harm." Well, as long as you are not playing any seriously *wrong* notes, you will be doing no musical harm! Once you have the *correct* thing down, *then* you can be more adventurous, creative and inspired! As John Coltrane once said, "The more you know, the more you can create." And I would venture to say that he knew what he was talking about!

Some might say that there is no such thing as a *wrong* note, there are only wrong ways to *play* them – wrong places to *put* them – wrong ways to insert them melodically into the harmonic structure one happens to be improvising on at the moment. And there is a lot of truth in that.

But in any case, a rock-solid knowledge of the *exact notes* that make up *every chord you are likely to see* as a jazz player is a great foundation on which to build solos of real and lasting musical value.

Another – and probably the *most* important thing to remember – is that, harmonically speaking, *everything is interrelated.* Every (major) scale has 7 notes, and 7 modes, which means that every note of every scale is part of 6 other scales, and (if you multiply 6 times 7) 42 other modes! And that is not even counting the non-diatonic scales, of which there are plenty!

And of course, every note can be part of a great number of chords. And the degree of the chord that that note is functioning as (along with the type of chord itself) will determine what I like to call its *harmonic color*. I tend to think of the basic tones of a chord...root, third, fifth, seventh... as the primary colors, and the ninth, eleventh, thirteenth, and various alterations (b5, #5, b9, #9) as the more exotic harmonic shades! But the interesting thing is that *every note has the same number of possible uses, harmonically speaking, as every other*! The relationships, relative to each possible chord and bass note, will stay the same!

We are going to go over a LOT of harmonic possibilities in this book, and I hope that it will greatly increase your knowledge and understanding not only of your particular instrument but of music and jazz playing in general. Have fun!

NOTE: For those of you who have *The Serious Jazz Practice Book* (or those who haven't got it... yet!) I would recommend a thorough review of the Diatonic 7th Chords and Arpeggio sections—in all keys—as a prelude to, or accompaniment for, this book.

ANOTHER NOTE: For those readers who would like to get right into practicing and playing, you are permitted to skip the painstaking analysis and music theory contained in Section One and proceed directly to Sections Two, Three and Four. But I would definitely recommend that you come back and peruse this first section at some later date. I think you will find it quite interesting and informative. Fascinating, even. If I do say so myself! - B.F.

Let's get started by taking a look at the various harmonic possibilities of one note. Let's see how many different things a "C" can be!

SECTION I WHAT A 'C' CAN BE

PART 1 The Root of All 'C' Chords

 I wanted to start this book off with a bit of practical music theory... *quite* a bit, actually... and discuss the incredible number of functions a single note can have. It can operate as a member of a tremendous variety of chords, and each chord that it functions as a part of will spin off its own arpeggio (which will *melodically define* that particular chord) and also, naturally, that chord's associated scale (or scales). This gives us an amazing number of choices, of harmonic and melodic avenues, musical roads that we can explore in different directions from our starting point, our central connection, our common tone, which in this case will be... you guessed it... C!

You can see quite easily in the first example how our C in the middle of the treble clef can be the tonic in a C major triad. I am sure you will be able to imagine playing a C major arpeggio against that C major chord, as well as the scale choices C major or C lydian. (The scales are written descending here so you can hear how they sound coming off the C in the middle of the staff; naturally they can be played up, down, intervallically, any way you choose!)

But obviously there are quite a few more "C" chords than just the plain old major triad! Since we are starting at the beginning, there is the minor triad, which comes with an assortment of possible scale choices:

Staying with triads for a moment, there is C augmented and its companion whole tone scale; the altered 7th scale is also a choice here. (See following page.)

1

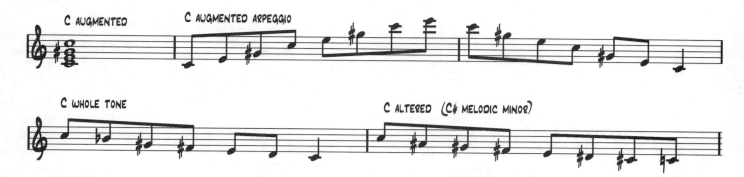

Then there are the various 7th chords built from C: C major 7th, whose scale choices are the same as for the major triad (C major and lydian, since the major 7th chord could be the tonic in C or the IV in G); C minor 7th (scales: natural minor, dorian, or phrygian, depending if the C minor 7th chord occurs in the modes of Eb, Bb, or Ab... are you following this?); C dominant 7th, where you would use the C mixolydian mode in the key of F (C7 is the V chord in that key); or, if you want the color of the #4, the C lydian dominant mode of the G melodic minor scale. There is Cm7b5, a chord which occurs as the VII chord in the key of Db (locrian mode), and also as the VI chord in the scale of Eb melodic minor, which is the scale you can use if you desire the harmonic color of the natural 9th (D natural in this case) against the Cm7b5 chord. (See following page.)

This was from an outdoor gig in Switzerland with the Crusaders in the early 80's. I used to like that t-shirt. And I wish I hadn't sold that guitar – my '59 sunburst Les Paul - I could pay off my mortgage with it today!.

There is C diminished 7th, with its symmetrical arpeggio and scale.

There are C major 7th(b5) and C major 7th(#5). It is worth noting that the latter chord can be regarded as an E major triad over a C. This concept of a triad over a (seemingly unrelated) bass note is very important and a preview of things that we will soon have to examine in depth!

And then there are the various alterations of the C dominant 7th chord: C7b5, C7#5, C7b9, C7#9, C7b5b9, #5#9, b5#9, #5b9....we will deal with most of these later in the book, because the best way to convey their special harmonic colors is to play them using mostly their *upper extensions*...and that is a whole other kettle of fish! (Play C in the bass as you play this next series of chords.)

(See following page)

Oh, and there is one more 7th chord, I almost forgot! Cm(major 7th), which conveys the sound of the first mode of the melodic minor scale.

Returning to three-note chords for a moment, there are the 3 perfect fourth quartal triads that can contain a C... and since each one of these can fit into the modes of 5 possible keys, they can have a multitude of possible harmonic uses - depending on the accompanying bass note, they can be analyzed every which way! But again, we will get into that subject later in the book. For now, we will present them analyzed from C.

You can see that there are a lot of ways to look at a C... simply from the *note* of C! That is to say, as the *tonic note* of various types of C chords.

But stay with me here... because we have just barely scratched the surface of our present task, which - I feel strangely compelled to remind you - is to explore all the things a C can be!

PART 2 An Integral Part of Seven Diatonic Scales and their Modes

Let's take a look at *modality* for another perspective on our note of choice. For example, in the key of C, our C will of course be the tonic (or 1) against the I chord, Cmajor7. But against the II chord Dm7, C will be the b7. Against the III (Em7) it will be the #5 (or b6), and against the IV chord, Fmaj7, the natural 5th. Against the V chord G7, it becomes the suspended 4th, which of course wants to resolve somewhere, usually down to the 3rd to make a G dominant 7th. C is the minor 3rd of the VI chord Am7, and against the VII chord Bm7b5, it is the b9... which makes it a note more fitting for a passing tone than a strong melody note against that particular chord. But it will resolve nicely to the note either above or below it.

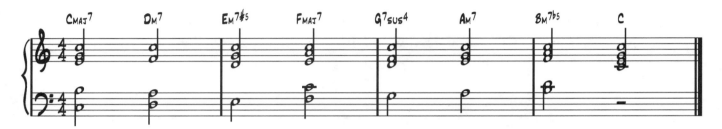

Here is an example using the C as the top note to lead into a melodic line made from the series of arpeggios that make up, in order (from 1 to 7), all the modal chords in the key of C:

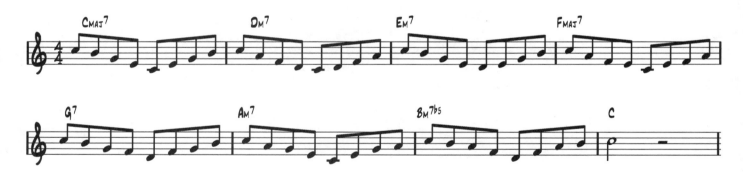

You can see (and hear) that *melodically*, our C has a slightly different *harmonic color* against each of the modal chords in the key of C, and therefore its *uses* against each of those particular chords will be slightly different, even if we are working *only* within the C major scale. In other words, against the Cmaj7, Dm7, Fmaj7, and Am7, the C is part of the *actual arpeggio* of the chord, but against the other 3 chords - Em7, G7, and Bm7b5 - the C functions more as a *passing tone* that wants to resolve to a *chord tone* - either to the B below it or the D above.

Let us not forget, however... that example only covers the *key* of C! But our C is a member of quite a few other clubs! There are 6 more diatonic scales that contain our versatile little note! Let's take a look at them, and see if we can get a feeling for the harmonic colors and possible uses of C in those other keys and their modes!

Let's add a flat to the key signature, making it the key of F. C is the fifth degree of that scale. This means that against the I chord Fmaj7 in that key, C is the 5th. But against the II chord, Gm7, it is the 4th, which creates a Gm11 sound. It is again the minor 3rd against the III chord Am7 (although the scale in this key would be the 3rd mode of F - A phrygian - not the 6th natural minor mode it would be in the key of C). Against the IV chord Bbmaj7 it is the 2nd (or 9th), making it a Bbmaj9 chord if added onto that. Against the V chord C7, it is... guess what?... the tonic! With the VI chord Dm7 it is again the b7, although here, in F, the scale would be the 6th mode, D natural minor, whereas in C it was the 2nd mode: D dorian. And finally, against the VII chord Em7b5, C is the #5 (or b6), a note that does not seem to be part of the chord unless you turn it upside down and analyze it *from* C.... then you realize that the notes of Em7b5 - E, G, Bb, and D - are the top 4 notes of a C7(9) chord!

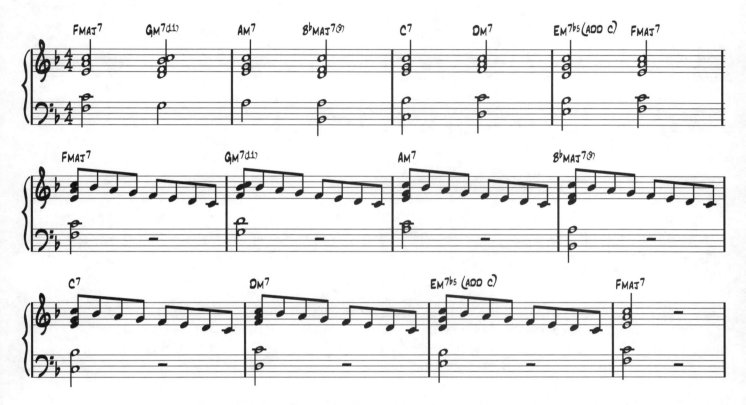

A good way to get a feeling for the colors of the C within the modes of the F (or any) scale is to play the scale descending (or ascending) from C against each of the modal chords. Of course, it is always a good idea to practice using the note in combination with the modal arpeggios as well.

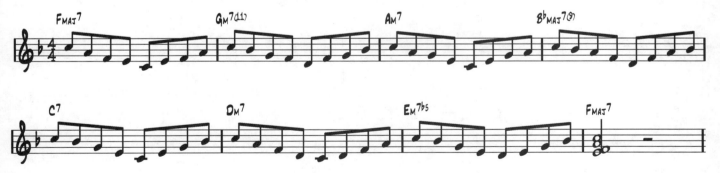

This will help maintain your *melodic perspective* in whatever key you happen to be playing in. And speaking of that, we still need to examine the vital part that our C can and does play in the other keys! We have to know all the places it can go, under what conditions, and how it gets there! It's a process of discovery that is only achieved through painstaking analysis. But once it is internalized, and the knowledge is not only understood but *heard*, we will be well on our way to mastering a very important aspect of improvising: *knowing exactly where we stand and what our options are no matter what harmonic context we are in at the moment!*

Anyway, back to work! In the key of G (one sharp), C will be the 4th - that begs for resolution down to the 3rd - against the I chord Gmaj7. In fact, C will be a serious *tension note* against several of the modal chords in this key, due to the fact that it is the 7th note of the V chord, D dominant 7th. It is the minor 3rd against the II chord Am7, but against the III chord, Bm7, it is the b9, making it little more than a passing tone in phrygian mode. It does become the tonic of the IV chord Cmaj7, and as previously mentioned, it is the b7 of D7. Against the VI chord Em7 it is the #5(b6), and the b5 against the VII chord F#m7b5.

And here is another arpeggiated example:

OK. Four more keys to go! Let's analyze them and see what C might be doing there! It is worth noting (pun intended!) that as the modal chords ascend up their scale degrees, the function of the C will be descending *downward*. Just another little thing to think about... the mathematical nature of music, symmetry, vibrations, etc.

For example, in Bb (2 flats) C is the major 9th against the Imaj7 chord, the tonic of the IIm7, the b7th against the IIIm7, the 6th against the IVmaj7, the 5th against the Vdom7, the 4th (11th) against the VIm7, and the minor 3rd against the VIIm7b5!

In Eb major (3 flats) C will be the 6th against Imaj7, the 5th against IIm7, and the 4th (11th) against IIIm7. In the IV chord Abmaj7 it is the major 3rd, and with the V chord Bb7, it is the 9th, forming a Bb9 chord! It is the tonic of the natural minor VI chord Cm7, and the b7th of the VII chord Dm7b5.

In Ab (4 flats) C becomes the major 3rd of Imaj7, the 9th (forming a Bbm9 chord) against IIm7, and the tonic of IIIm7. It is the major 7th of the IV chord Dbmaj7, and the 6th (13th) of the V chord Eb7... some nice tonal colors here. It is the 5th of VIm7 and the 4th (11th) of VIIm7b5.

Next is another example of how to make a melody from the modal arpeggios, this time turning them around a little and throwing in some motivic development:

And finally, in Db (5 flats) C is the major 7th of the I chord Dbmaj7. Against the IIm7 it is the major 6th, which creates an Ebm7(13) chord. Nice. It is the 5th of IIIm7, just an ordinary chord tone, but against the IVmaj7 it is the #4 (#11) (the tone unique to the lydian mode) and makes it a Gbmaj7(#11) chord. It is the major 3rd of the V chord Ab dominant 7th, the 9th of the VI (Bbm7), and last but not least, it is the tonic of the VII chord Cm7b5!

And again, an example of how the C could function melodically within the arpeggios of the modal chords in the key of Db:

So, there you have it. One note, functioning as part of 7 different keys, and more importantly, functioning with wonderfully different *uses and harmonic colors* within each of the modal scales and against each of the modal chords contained in those 7 keys. And remember, every note has the *exact same relationships*, mathematically *and* musically, throughout all the keys it is part of, as every other! It is a solid musical concept and one that, once mastered, will provide a great springboard from which to jump further into the ocean of harmonic possibilities!

But we are not finished with our explorations here... not by a long shot! Let's complete our theoretical preparation for the rest of this book by seeing how many ways a "C" can be analyzed and used in different harmonic contexts that were not included in the first two sections.

PART 3 A Part of Chords Built from Every Possible Bass Note

We already have covered most of the different types of "C" chords one is likely to see in a jazz context... that is, chords using C as the *bass note*. But now, let us use C as our *lead melody note* in chords with *different bass notes*. There will be quite a few varieties of chords built from each possible bass note, even though the relationship between the C and the bass note of choice will *stay the same*. For example, the C will always be the major 7th of Db... but there will be several different chord possibilities within that relationship, each one dictating its own scale *and* its own arpeggio!

Let's stay with that idea and go right up the chromatic scale with our bass notes, putting our "C" on top, and see what we get!

Starting, as we said, with Db in the bass, C is the major 7th. So the first chord we would probably think of is a Dbmaj7, which would dictate the straight Db major scale. But let's play it down from C. Of course, another possibility would be Dbmaj7b5, which would call for the Db lydian scale (the 4th mode of Ab major). But let's play that scale down from C as well. We can raise the 5th, creating a Dbmaj7#5, in which case the scale becomes Bb melodic minor. Playing the scale down from C lets us hear and become familiar with the *harmonic color* of the C against each chord and within each of the scales! We can put the perfect 5th back in and flat the 3rd, making it a Dbm(maj7), which calls for the Db melodic minor scale. And lastly, there are the diminished scale-based chords C/Db and Am/Db.

You can look at the last two chords as triads of C major and Am respectively over the Db bass note, but I also like to call them Dbdim(extended) and (double extended) because they are made by extending one or both of the top two notes of the basic diminished 7th chord. (There is more on them and their melodic uses in *The Serious Jazz Practice Book*.)

Before we move on, let's play through the arpeggios of the chords we just discussed, using the C as the pivotal note. This will serve us well in our future explorations. Remember - this book is about the *harmonic* possibilities of melodic playing! You might want to play each chord briefly before playing its arpeggio.

All right, then. On to the bass note of D! C is the minor 7th against the D. So obviously we can make D7 (mixolydian or lydian dominant), Dm7 (dorian, phrygian, or natural minor), Dm7b5 (locrian), and Dm7#5 (phrygian or natural minor) chords with C in the lead. Dm9 (dorian or natural minor) and assorted sus4 chords are also readily available: D7sus and C/D (mixolydian, dorian, or natural minor, depending on whether it resolves to a dom7 or m7 chord) and Dm7(11).

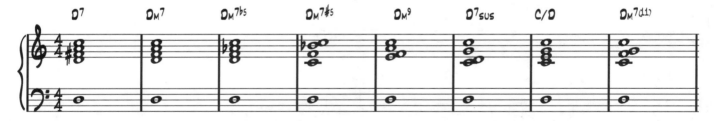

There are also D7b9 (diminished or altered), D7b5 (whole tone, diminished or altered), D7#5 (whole tone or altered), as well as one of my favorites, Ab/D, which can be analyzed as D7b5b9 (minus the major 3rd F#) since Ab is the b5 and Eb the b9! The scale choices for that one are diminished and altered. And of course there are the other alterations of the dom7th chords, D7b5#9 (diminished or altered), D7#5#9 and D7#5b9 (altered). Notice that just as D7b5b9 is mostly an *Ab major triad over D*, the D7b5#9 is an *F minor triad over D* (although it does help to have the F# in the lower part of the chord on that one). This is a preview of things to come!

And here are the scales we just discussed, all played down from C, with some little reminders of their parent scales. Remember that the diminished scale will have its root a half step above the dominant 7th chord it is being played over. That is why many jazz players refer to the second mode of the diminished scale, the one *beginning with the root* of the 7th chord(s), as the "half-step" diminished scale!

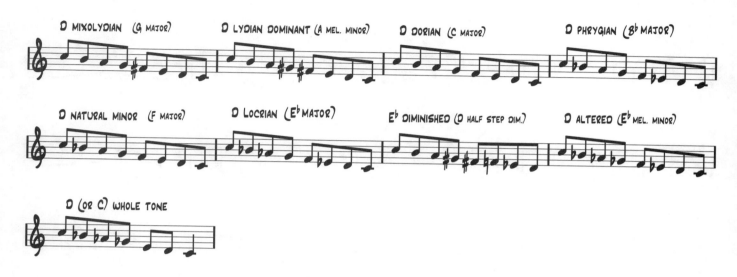

This is from 1977, °I think, the "Heavy Metal Bebop" tour with the Brecker Bros. I was playing the Guitorganizer – it was a Les Paul Black Beauty with wired frets and was a guitar, organ and synthesizer rolled into one!

And let's not forget those arpeggios!

Man! As they say in the trade, that is some bad-ass shit! The simpler arpeggios are pretty straight ahead and easy to hear, but as the complexity of the altered 7th chords increases, you can see that some very interesting melodic possibilities arise from stating the *exact notes of the alterations* in their arpeggios!

OK. We move now to chords with C in the lead over the bass note of Eb. C is the major 6th of Eb, and of course the 13th if we are dealing with the upper extensions of a chord. The simplest chord here would be a plain Eb(6), also analyzable as a Cm7 over Eb. We can put the quartal triad of D-G-C over the Eb bass note, creating a maj7 chord with the 6th on top; this chord is usually called a maj7(6). The other two perfect 4th quartal triads are also possibilities here, creating two varieties of an Eb6/9 chord. And we can put an F major triad over the Eb, a chord you can look at as an F7 chord with the 7th in the bass, or an Eb lydian chord containing the degrees of 6-9-#11. All the above chords could be soloed on using either major or lydian scale, except the last one, F/Eb, which would be lydian only!

Those would pretty much be the *major* chord possibilities here. If we put a minor 3rd in the chord, we can make an Ebm13 or Ebm6/9 with the C in the lead (dorian) or an Eb diminished (I'll leave it to you to guess what scale goes with that one...hint: who's buried in Grant's tomb?) Interestingly, against the Ebm13, the Eb *half-step diminished scale* (Db regular diminished) is also an option.

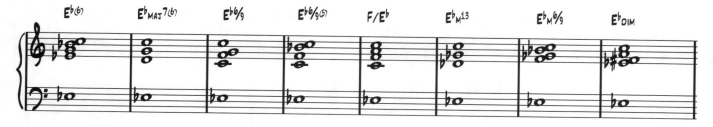

Actually, I don't think I need to write out each individual scale for every chord anymore. You know what they are... if there is one you are confused about, just go to the chord/scale index in the back of the book and look it up! However, I do think it is important to play through the arpeggios of each chord we are constructing and discussing here!

16

There are a few more chords to be made over Eb with C in the lead, and I wanted to discuss them separately because what we are going to see here is some *overlapping* with most of the chords we made earlier over the bass note Db, namely Dbmaj7, Dbmaj7b5, Dbmaj7#5, and the diminished (extended and double extended) polychords C/Db and Am/Db.

I want you to pay particular attention here because this is the first example of one of the most important principles in this book: *multiple uses of the same harmonic materials*! The chords that over Db were variations of the Db major 7th and diminished chords take on a whole new character when placed over the Eb bass note! And playing the *same* arpeggios - *melodically* - within the *new harmonic context*, can open up a world of very hip shit!

For example, Dbmaj7 over Eb becomes an Eb13sus, containing the degrees b7-9-11-13. Resolve the Ab to G and we get a straight Eb13 chord. It's basically a II-V progression over the bass note of Eb (you would use the Eb mixolydian scale against the II-V here). Raise the Ab in the first chord to A natural, and we get another type of V chord in our II-V: an Eb13 with a #11! Here you would switch from Eb mixolydian to Eb lydian dominant on the V chord to include the color of the #11. Go back to the Eb13sus and change to the C/Db over the Eb bass...that makes it an Eb13b9! And if you resolve the Eb13sus to the Am/Db over the Eb bass, it's an Eb13b5b9! (Go from Eb mixolydian to the Db diminished scale [Eb half-step] for those last two progressions.)

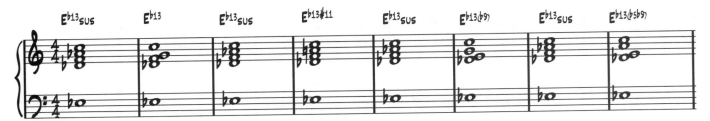

And here is an example, using a little bit of melodic development, of how one might use the arpeggios of the chords in the four variations of the II-V progression we just discussed.

Lots of possibilities already covered, and we are still just a little way in! Let's look at E as the bass note with C in the lead. C against E is the #5 and/or b6. The first chord that comes to mind is a C triad with the third in the bass, C/E (Cmajor). Also the E (or C or G#) augmented triad (whole tone or altered). Another possibility is C-G-D, the quartal triad again, making it an Em7#5 (also known as C2/E - E phrygian). Add the major 3rd above the bass note and we have an E7#5#9 (altered). Drop the G to F# and it is an E9#5 (whole tone), and drop it once more down to F and it becomes an E7#5b9 (altered). The other commonly used jazz chords that occur to me here are F/E and Fmaj7/E (phrygian) and Edim7(extended) with the C on top (diminished). This last chord is sometimes referred to as an Eb13b9 with the b9 in the bass. (See following page.)

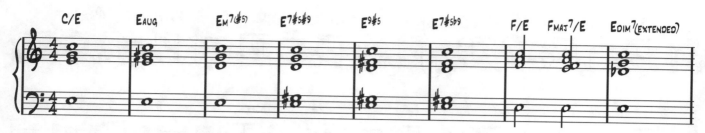

Shall we arpeggiate them? I can't think of a good reason why not!

Moving on... in chords with F in the bass, C is the perfect 5th. Clearly there will be a bunch of chord possibilities here. Why don't we arrange them in a way that makes a little bit of musical sense? Starting with F major triad, we can drop the tonic note chromatically so it makes a maj7, dom7, and 6th chord, then becoming a Dbmaj7#5 over F. Notice that the top 3 notes (the 3-#5-7) of this Db chord are an F major triad! We can begin our downward chromatic motion again from the #5, making a Dbmaj7, Dbmaj7b5, and switch to a Gbmaj7b5 when the G goes down to Gb. Then let's continue down from the tonic of the F minor triad, making Fm(maj7), m7, and m6. Next we can do a Cm7/F (which is also an F9sus) to F7b9, resolving to Bb major, then minor, and a few more utterly marvelous chords: F7#9, Fm6/9 (also an Abmaj7b5 over F!), Ebm13/F, and finally a turnaround chord, C7b9 over F, resolving to C/F, which is an Fmaj9 without the 3rd!

Wow. That's quite a nice little chord progression! It occurs to me that one fun way to play with the arpeggios of these chords would be to make them into a montuno type of thing. Something like this, perhaps: (See following page.)

That was nice, wasn't it? A good example of how you can use arpeggios to take *melodic control* over the prevailing harmony! But let's not get too pleased with ourselves just yet...we still have a lot of work to do!

Let's see what we can do with our C in the lead over the bass note of Gb (F#). C is the b5 (or #4) against Gb. That forms a tritone. Each tritone is part of two dominant 7th chords... not coincidentally, a tritone apart! So the first chords I would think of here are D7/F# and its tritone-substitution relative Ab/Gb... which could be seen as Ab with the 7th in the bass or as a Gb lydian chord closely related to our next entry, Gbmaj7b5! There are also Gb7b5 and its dominant 7th variations: Gb9(#11) whose top 3 notes are an *augmented triad*; Gb13(#11), which is an *Ab triad* superimposed over the Gb7 lower structure; Gb7b5b9 (*C triad* in the upper structure); and Gb7b5#9 (*Am triad*). And then there are Gbm7b5 (whose top 3 notes also comprise an Am triad) and Gbdim7. And one more chord that you could look at as a variation on diminished(extended), since it extends the Eb in the Gbdim7 chord up to an F - F/Gb!

For our arpeggiation example this time, let's play around with each one for 2 bars and over a 2 octave range. And let's try to accentuate the triads in the upper structure of the chords that contain them as much and as clearly as possible!

(See following page)

19

Only 5 more bass notes to go! Let's have a look at G in the bass with C (here the 4th or 11th) in the lead. Something tells me we are going to see a lot of sus chords! And we do...Gsus, G7sus, Gm7sus, F/G, Fmaj7/G, Dm7/G, Gm11, all closely related chords. Also Gm7b5sus which, interestingly, is a Dbmaj7b5 over G, or it could also be the top part of an Eb13 without the root! You can look at its neighbor, Dbmaj7#5 over G, as a Gm7b5sus with a *natural 9*, or an Eb13#11! We will see some more uses of these chords when we get to the bass note of A... but I don't want to give them away just yet. I think I'll keep you in *sus-pense* a little longer!

Back to simplicity with a C/G, C7/G, C13/G, Cm/G, Cm7/G, Cm6/G...we don't need to list every last C/G chord here, but since G is the 5th of C, just about any C chord without an altered 5th will work against the G bass. We can also put the C in the lead of an Ab triad over G, and its sister chords Abmaj7, Abmaj7b5 and Abmaj7#5 sound very hip and jazzy over the G as well!

And we can also put the C at the top of a Gdim7 (extended) or (double extended). These diminished scale-based chords can be analyzed every which way. The former could be an Eb13b9 or an A7#9, the latter an Eb13#9 or an A13#9, without roots, among others!

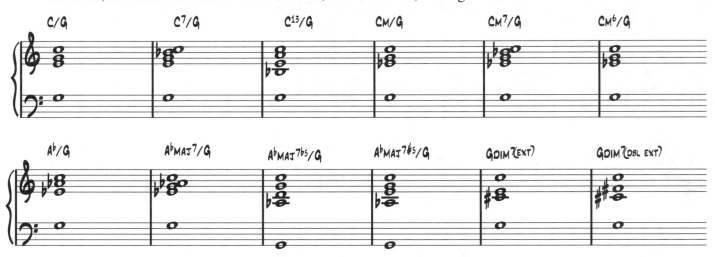

Please try to keep in mind, as you go through these examples, that if you can train yourself to automatically go *directly to the arpeggio notes* of a chord *as soon as you see the chord symbol*, you will definitely be one step ahead of the game when it comes to creating musically valid and compelling melodies!

Let's move the bass note up to Ab. C in the lead becomes the major 3rd. So we can do Ab major, augmented, 6th, and maj7th chords, including maj7b5, maj7#5 (notice: that one is a C triad over Ab), 6/9 and maj7/6. We also have all the variations of Abdom7 - 7b5, 7#5, 9, 7b9,13, 13b9 (an F triad over Ab7), 7b5b9 (which contains a D triad), and two similar 7sus chords: Ab7sus(3) and Gbmaj7#11/Ab. I am leaving out the chords here that contain a #9... even though the C is technically part of those chords, the major 3rd doesn't sound that great in the lead with a #9 (minor 3rd) underneath it. (With the possible exception of Ab#5#9.)

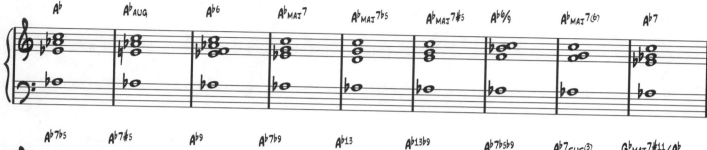

And again, let's arpeggiate those chords, keeping in mind the goal of doing it in a very musical... and melodic... way! Notice that in several places (Ab6/9, Ab9, Ab13) the tonic (Ab) and sometimes the 5th (Eb) are left out of the arpeggios completely, and we are playing only the *upper extensions*. This is an important concept to keep in mind!

22

Next we have the bass note of A, with C becoming the minor 3rd above it. The most obvious chord we would think of here would be Am triad, and - as we did in previous examples - we can move the tonic downward chromatically in a typical minor chord progression, going to Am(maj7) (there's that augmented triad again, this time over A), Am7, Am6, and when the F# goes down to F, an Fmaj7 (or Dm9 without the root) over A. Replace the A with a G and we have Am7#5. Then there are Am7b5 (a Cm triad over A) and Adim7 (which could be the V chord of a II-V here since it is also a D7b9 without the root!), and its dim(extended) relative Ab/A. F7/A is another possibility here.

Of course, in A chords that already contain a major 3rd, C would become the #9. So we can make A7#9 (with or without a 5th), A7b5#9, A7#5#9 (there's that Db [here C#] maj7b5 again, and if we put the 7th in the lower register, C#maj7#5!), and one of my personal favorites, A13#9 (which is a Gdim[double extended] over A).

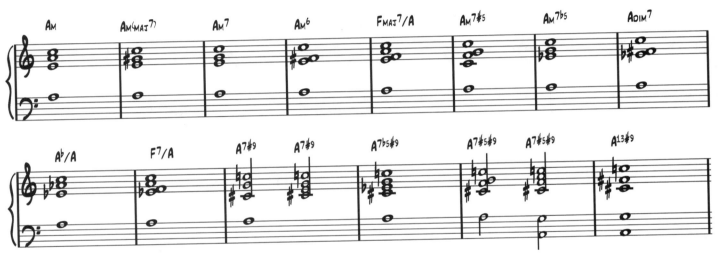

In Japan with the Crusaders, 1980... I had arrived at my hotel room and this brand new SG guitar was sitting on the bed with a bouquet of flowers... a gift from Yamaha!

And let's take another step toward achieving melodic command of these chords! How, you might ask? Well, it certainly never hurts to play their arpeggios up and down your instrument... it's really the only way to thoroughly learn all the notes involved!

Only a couple more bass notes to go... don't lose your concentration now! Here we go with Bb against which C is the 2nd (or 9th). There will be major, minor, dominant and diminished possibilities here. In the major category we have two varieties of Bb(2): the 1-2-5 quartal triad and the major triad with an added 2nd. We have two kinds of Bbmaj9: the standard version 3-5-7-9 (which is a Dm7/Bb), and F/Bb (the same chord with no 3rd). There are the other two quartal triads which make Bb6/9 and Bbmaj7/6. And there are the lydian chords C/Bb and Am/Bb (technically 6/9/#11 and maj7/9/#11 respectively).

In the minor category, there are Bbm9, Bbm6/9 and Bbm9(maj7)... and what do you know, here come those Db chords again - Dbmaj7, maj7b5 and maj7#5 - didn't we just play those last two over A?? Well, here they are over Bb! We can also make Bbm9(13), Bbm9(#5), and a close modal relative of that one, Gbmaj7b5/Bb. And let us not forget Bbm7b5(9)... the top part of which comprises a Dbm(maj7)!

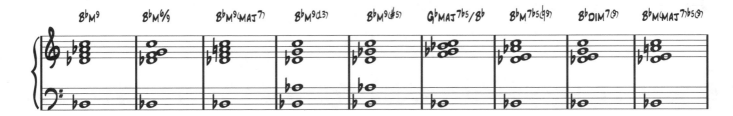

And if we drop the 5th (Ab) in that last Db chord to G, we get a dim(extended) chord - C triad over Db - that could be analyzed here as Bbdim7(9). If we raise the Ab to A it becomes a dim(double extended) that would be - what? A Bbm(maj7)b5 with a 9th on top?? Could be. But don't worry... it's really just another diminished scale-based chord.

And in the dominant 7th category, there are Bb(9), Bb9(b5) and Bb9(#5). These last two, since they contain both the 9th *and* the b5 or #5, are whole tone scale-based. There is one of my favorites, Bb9(#11-13), which is actually a C major triad over the Bb7 lower structure. And there are the varieties of Bb7(sus), including Ab/Bb, Abmaj7/Bb and Fm7/Bb.

Well, now. That's a lot of chords there! And I am sure you are noticing that we are seeing a lot of repeats of chords we already covered with the other bass notes underneath them. The upper structures, including the major and quartal triads, the Dbmaj7 chord alterations, etc. *remain the same*. Only their *uses* and *tonal colors* change *within each new harmonic context, i.e. over each new bass note*!

So I am not going to write out a lengthy arpeggiated example of each chord this time. What I want *you* to do (and this will be a good preparation for what we are going to do later in the book) is to *look* at each chord, and as you are looking at it, play the arpeggio up and down the full range of your instrument. Then... start playing around with the notes. Turn them around. Reverse their direction. Make some phrases out of them... three-note groups, 4-note groups, whatever. Find some melodic phrases that *work* for you on your particular axe! And I want you to do that with every one of the chords in the last section!

I'll give you one example of what I am talking about, on Bb9. *(See next page.)*

And now we come to our last possible bass note from which to analyze and build chords with our "C" on top: B! C against B is the b9. We can make a C/B, which could be a Cmaj7 with the 7th in the bass, and/or a phrygian modal chord that wants to resolve down to the B. There is Am/B, a nice substitution for F#m7b5/B (of which Am is the top 3 notes) when resolving to B7. There is F/B, which could still be a C major scale-based chord (F lydian) but sounds more like B7b5b9, which it totally becomes when we add the major 3rd D# (Eb), making it also an F7/B. Then there is B7#5b9, which if you look at it another way is Am7b5 over B, or Cm triad over B7. And finally we have the diminished scale-based B7b9 and B13b9, a dim(extended) chord which as you can see is an Ab triad over the B7 lower structure.

For this last example we are going to play the arpeggios up and their associated scale (or scales) down. This is also a good way to get a feel for the *complete tonality* of each chord.

So now we have done it! We have taken a single note - C - and examined it from a great variety of angles! You can see that the sounds and uses of a note can continually change, depending on the scale, the mode, the chord it is a part of. And *real awareness* of what the *melodic* possibilities are from any note one is playing - *through any harmonic context* - is crucial for the modern jazz soloist! Melody informed by - and capable of *clearly stating* - the harmony! That is what we are going for here!

A little later, we are going to do the same thing with each common chord form... that is, analyze each one from every possible bass note. We saw a lot of examples of that in this section, but it is very important to thoroughly train your brain! We are setting very high goals here. So this is the advice I would offer you at this time:

Analyze, analyze, analyze! Just do it - until it becomes automatic! Analyze every chord and *every note in them* every possible way you can! Think of how many different things each one can be! That's the only way one can take advantage of *all* their possible uses.

But also keep in mind that once you are done analyzing... it's time to play!

PART 4 Harmonic Rhythm and Harmonic Regions

Harmonic rhythm is an easy concept to understand. It has to do with the duration of chords and the points where they change. The number of beats (or bars) that each chord occupies in the structure of a tune determines that tune's harmonic rhythm. In tunes in 4/4 time, generally speaking, chords will change either on the first beat or the third beat of the bar. In many cases, of course, some chords will last for one, two, or more bars. And occasionally, a chord will change on a different beat, such as the 2 or 4. A good example of all those harmonic rhythm possibilities can be seen in the chord changes of Joe Henderson's classic, "Recordame".

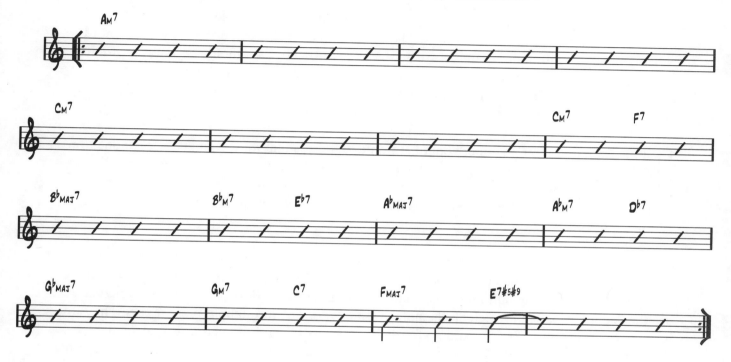

As we can see, the first chord, Am7, lasts for 4 bars, and the next one, Cm7, lasts for 3 bars and 2 beats before changing to F7 on the 3rd beat of the 8th bar. Then the harmonic rhythm shifts... to one full bar of Bbmaj7, two beats each for the II-V Bbm7-Eb7... then repeats that same harmonic rhythm twice: one bar Abmaj7, two beats each Abm7-Db7, one bar Gbmaj7, two beats each Gm7-C7 (notice here that the *harmonic rhythm* - chords falling on the 1st and 3rd beats of the bar - is repeated, *not the chord sequence*...if the chord sequence had continued downward that would have made it Gbm7-B7!). And finally, a little rhythmic variation: two dotted quarter notes (3 beats total) of Fmaj7 and a change to E7#9 on the 4th beat, which continues into the final bar!

So what exactly does this mean? Well, basically, it just means that this is where the chords change in the song. That this is how long they last. Sometimes the harmonic rhythm is long and drawn out, as in the first 8 bars. And sometimes it moves faster, as in the second part of the tune.

Sometimes the harmonic rhythm moves faster still, with the chords changing on every beat. Thankfully for the modern jazz soloist, this usually happens on slower tunes! Duke Ellington's "Sophisticated Lady" is a good example of this:

(See following page)

So, chords change on certain beats. And the beats that they change on determine the harmonic rhythm. That much should be clear now. And for the *number* of beats, or bars, that that chord is being played, a *harmonic region* is created! My definition of a harmonic region is a certain length of time within a tune where *one chord* is being played. So every chord change in every tune carries its own harmonic region with it. In "Sophisticated Lady" the first harmonic region lasts for a full bar, the next four last for one beat apiece, and so on.

The important thing to remember about harmonic regions is that for the length of each one, for the duration of each chord change, it is the *notes of that chord* that will be the bedrock, the most solid foundation for improvisation by the modern jazz soloist! (Of course, we will have many choices to make of what *kind* of chord - what upper extensions, what alterations, etc. - to use within each harmonic region.)

On "Recordame", one might picture the harmonic regions something like this: Since the first 4 bar section is all Am7, one could choose the Am7 arpeggio or its next two extensions, Cmaj7 or Em7, that are formed by building thirds (in Am) from the C and E respectively. Or one could just use the A dorian scale, in which all the notes would work fine throughout those 4 bars. The same idea - taken up a minor 3rd - would go for the next 3 bars of the Cm7 chord. But when the harmonic rhythm shifts and the II-V-I progressions start coming every 2 bars, the harmonic regions will be more sharply defined.

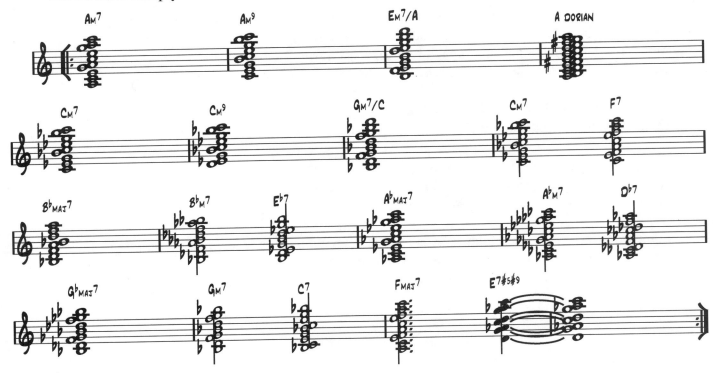

The point of this is that if, when soloing, we make our note choices from these *specific arpeggios*, within the *exact duration* of each harmonic region (i.e. chord change) we can do so in any order, with *any phrasing*, and our playing will be harmonically rock-solid!

And if we made the choice, for example - when the II-V-I's start happening every two bars - to substitute *IIm9-Vdom7#5-Imaj9* instead of the straight m7-dom7-maj7, we might come up with something like this (starting from bar 7 of the tune):

Another very useful option to keep in mind when dealing with arpeggios is *approach notes*. We can use a chromatic approach from below or the applicable scale tone from above to get to any note in a chord's arpeggio (there are a bunch of exercises dealing with this in *The Serious Jazz Practice Book*). This can add some nice melodic tension and diversity to our improvisations while keeping them harmonically strong!

Here are a couple of examples in Bb minor.

And let's try some of that same stuff on "Sophisticated Lady":

We can see that by focusing on the arpeggio of the chord in each harmonic region, either by using chord notes exclusively or by adding approach notes to them, we can have a great deal of *melodic flexibility* while still retaining total *harmonic control* over our improvisations. Which is what this book is really all about!

But there will surely be times when your imagination calls for playing more than just the arpeggios and their approach notes in your solos. You will probably want at times to accentuate color notes, utilize passing tones, make use of all the different scales and upper extensions that can apply to any particular chord. In any case, you will want to get the most out of all the melodic materials that are available to you. And you will want to do it in a way that is *harmonically strong*!

And that brings us to one of the most important ideas in this book.

PART 5 The Concept of the Strong Beats

In our recent discussion of harmonic rhythm, we talked about the beats on which chords change - in 4/4 time, usually on the 1 and/or the 3. But *whether or not* the chords are changing every two beats, the ONE and the THREE are the STRONG BEATS in 4/4 time (unless the tempo is slow enough to call for 16th notes, in which case the TWO and FOUR could also be regarded as strong beats). In 3/4 time, it's just the ONE (possibly again, if 16th notes are involved, also the TWO and THREE). The strong beats (other than the ONE) vary in other time signatures, depending on the subdivisions. But we are going to talk mainly about 4/4 time here.

The STRONG BEATS are the beats that keep the time and hold the groove together - ONE, two, THREE, four, ONE, two, THREE, four. And to the ear of the listener, they are the *most important beats to accent* when it comes to *stating (or implying)* the harmony!

We already have seen how arpeggios, with or without approach notes, can be used to melodically state the harmony of any chord. But if we can be sure to place a *chord note* on each STRONG BEAT, we will be able to do almost anything else in between, while still retaining the overall *harmonic strength* of our improvisation! Here are some examples, first just on single chords (you might do something like this on a chord that lasted one or more bars):

On Cm7, we place a chord tone on every strong beat ONE and THREE (accented) with chromatic passing tones in between.

On Bbmaj7b5, we do the same thing but stay within the Bb lydian modal scale.

On Abm7b5, again we put chord tones on the strong beats with chromatic passing tones.

If the chords are changing on every bar, we would want to put chord tones on the two strong beats in each one. Then we would otherwise be free to use either scale notes or chromatic passing tones to noodle around them! (See following page.)

If a chord is anticipated, we can put a chord tone on the anticipation, like on the last beat of this one:

And of course, if the chords are changing every two beats (or quicker), we will only need one strong beat chord tone per change. We have to keep in mind where we are going, though, because those harmonic regions will be shifting fast! Here's an example on the changes of John Coltrane's "Moment's Notice", which I strongly suspect was so entitled because that's how long you have to think about switching keys while playing on it!

While we can see that placing a chord tone on every strong beat will definitely help make melodies that clearly state what the harmony is doing, there is no absolute rule that it necessarily *has* to be a chord tone. The main thing is for the soloist to take harmonic control of the situation! Approach notes will also do nicely on the strong beats, as in this example on the first 8 bars of the same song:

Of course, we can also look at the idea of approach notes like this: every note you play is going to be approaching some other note...from somewhere!

In fact, the strong beats can be used to emphasize and accent any color note, chord alteration or upper extension that we choose, and make them stand out in the overall melodic and harmonic scheme of the moment! The only thing required is *awareness of the sound and use* of our chosen note(s) against the chord(s) in question. This would include the knowledge of what scales and/or arpeggios the note we are accenting on the strong beat could be part of.

For example, here's a II-V-I progression in C, starting with D dorian over the Dm7 going up to an E(the 13th) on the first strong beat of the G7, then descending down the (G7 half step) diminished scale, which accents the Bb (the #9) on the second strong beat.

Or we can do the same thing, but when we get to the E, we can play a descending E major triad, which makes a G13b9 chord out of the diminished scale!

We could also play the D dorian up, then choose to accent the Eb - the #5(b6) - on the first strong beat of G7, which would call for the G7 altered scale (or possibly whole tone). Here we will go with the altered, and throw in a G augmented arpeggio at the end before coming to rest on D (the 9th) on the first strong beat of Cmaj7.

Or we could put the 9th on the two strong beats of the Dm7 chord, outlining a Dm9 (Fmaj7) arpeggio, before going to an Ab (the b9) on the first G7 strong beat, which gives us a springboard to play the rest of the Db major triad - for a moment giving us a G7b5b9 chord - before resolving out of G7 altered to the 9th of Cmaj7 again, then arpeggiating that chord and finally coming to rest on a lovely color note, F# (the #11).

Once we know what the *primary voice movement* is within a chord progression, we can use the strong beats to *melodically* accent that movement! Here's a II-V-I (in Eb) with a typical descending line in the II (minor) chord, going from the tonic-maj7-minor7 of F minor to the 3rd of the V chord Bb7, then a little chromatic twist on the Ebmaj7 with the accent on the #11.

And here is a relative of the last progression: Bb13sus(Abmaj7/Bb) to Bb13#11(Abmaj7#5/Bb), back to the Bb13sus and then down to a Bb13b9. Notice that if we look at the Bb13sus as an Fm7/Bb (it is actually an Fm9), the movement is almost the same as the Fm-Fm(maj7)-Fm7-Bb7 in the previous example!

Here's another common voice movement, this time in A minor, with the E (the 5th) in the A minor triad moving up chromatically to make it a minor #5, then a minor 6th, finally going down again to become the #5 of an A7 altered chord resolving to D minor. Notice the minor chord *color notes* (9 and 11) and the *altered notes* on the strong beats of the 7th chord here.

Speaking of primary voice movement, it is worthwhile to mention that in that most common of chord progressions, the II-V, the most important voices (other than the bass notes) are the *3rds and 7ths* of both chords. When the bass note changes from 2 to 5, the *b3* of the IIm7 becomes the *b7* of the Vdom7 chord as the *b7* of the IIm7 moves down a half step, becoming the *3* of the Vdom7! Here's an example using two inversions of some chromatically descending II-V's:

So you can place those b7's and (flatted and major) 3rds on the strong beats of your solo and obtain some very strong and clear harmonic/melodic results!

There are a lot of choices for voice movements within the II-V chord progression. If we take the 5th of the IIm7 chord and move it down chromatically, it becomes the b9 of the Vdom7 chord. And if we take the *top 3 notes* of the IIm7 (the 3, 5, and b7) - which form a *major triad* - and move them down chromatically, they will become the 13, b9 and 3rd of the Vdom7, making it a 13b9 chord. But it is actually just major triads moving down chromatically that form the upper structure! Here are three II-V's going down in whole steps and finally resolving to a major 7th chord. (See following page.)

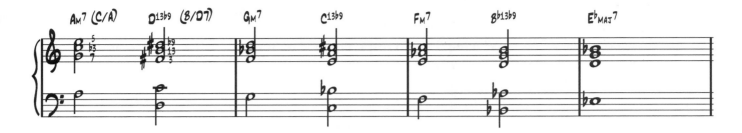

And of course we can use any of those 3 downward moving chromatic lines (from the notes of the descending major triads) to accent with the strong beats, as in this example using mostly the arpeggios of those triads:

Clearly, there are a lot more examples we could talk about here. But trust me: there is PLENTY of stuff coming up which will make *practical musical sense* out of all this. Harmonic rhythm. The concept of harmonic regions and their changing arpeggios. Approach notes and passing tones. Scale-based lines utilizing the strong beats to emphasize chord tones, color notes, and chord alterations. The understanding of all of these can be extremely valuable to the modern jazz soloist!

In any case, the important thing to remember about the STRONG BEATS is this: whatever *harmonic movement* is going on in any particular tune, or whatever *additional harmonic variations* one chooses to *superimpose* or *create*, it can be clearly *accented* and *defined* by the modern jazz soloist, if one knows which notes are the *most important* ones to stress - *melodically* - to *show* that harmonic movement! The strong beats are kind of like the dots that can be connected to tie our melodies together - with respect to both the harmony and the time!

I encourage you to re-read that last paragraph a few times. Understand it. Put it to use. Because THE CONCEPT OF THE STRONG BEATS, once mastered, will help you achieve complete harmonic, melodic, and improvisational command over every tune you will ever play!

SECTION II MASTERING THE CHANGES

PART 1 The Individual Chord

Before we get started here I feel compelled to remind you that there is a pretty thorough section on all the different types of arpeggios and ways to approach them melodically in *The Serious Jazz Practice Book*, and I would recommend going over them - *in all keys* - as much as possible - as a companion study to this book.

But OK. Let's take a look at a typical chord we might be likely to see in a tune: Bb7. When we see that chord, we would instinctively gravitate to its arpeggio, since we know that is the most effective way to melodically convey the sound of that chord:

Of course, however, we would not want to just run the arpeggio up and down. That would be melodically boring! But there are so many ways to break up and turn around those arpeggio notes - and more importantly, to add *motivic development* to them - that we can make an interesting melody without straying from our basic chord tones!

If we just *think rhythmically* - and restrict ourselves to chord notes - we can come up with some surprisingly good stuff!

And then if we start adding approach notes into the mix - chromatic from below, scale note from above - the melodic possibilities on that chord really start to open up! Notice here how when the approach notes land on the strong beats, some nice *melodic tension and color* is created.

Ultimately, we can utilize the entire scale vocabulary, from diatonic to chromatic, while always maintaining control of what chord or color tones we emphasize on the strong beats.

But of course, as we mentioned earlier, there will be plenty of times when the chords will be changing a lot quicker... every bar, every two beats, sometimes even every beat. At times like that, we will need to have *smaller melodic fragments* that can *strongly convey the sound of each chord* within the available space!

Now, obviously there are a LOT of choices and ways to do this. We have already discussed scales leading to chord tones on the strong beats, approach notes, etc. But the *strongest and clearest* way - and for starters, a *great* way to *practice* doing it - is to use *all arpeggio notes*, and break them up into 4-note groups. Returning to Bb7, here are the 4 possible inversions, played melodically:

It is easy to see how each one of those inversions can be melodically turned around and broken up in a number of different ways. Here are four examples on each of the inversions:

(See following page)

Mathematically there are a lot more ways to mess with them. If you play around with the voices of each inversion I'm sure you will discover some more! But as a very wise musician once said on the subject of chords, "It's not how they sound by *themselves*... it's how they go *together* that matters!"

Let's say that Bb7 chord is the V chord of a II-V progression. Fm7 would be the II chord, with each chord lasting for 2 beats. To continue our exercise here, we will need some 4-eighth-note bits of the Fm7 arpeggio, made from its inversions the same way we did previously with Bb7:

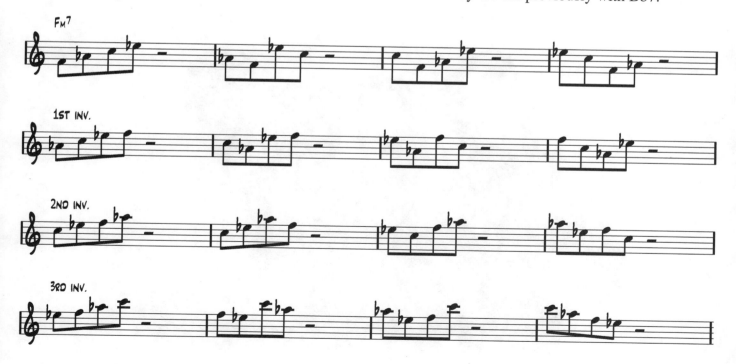

Then, it's kind of like a jazz version of a Chinese menu: choose one (4-note group) from column A (in this case the Fm7 bits) and one from column B (the Bb7 bits). Put them together and you have one bar of a perfectly melodically and harmonically stated II-V! Continue the process of putting different fragments together (possibly with an approach note or two to break up the monotony) and you will discover a great number of variations within the same theme: playing this particular progression - this II-V - melodically with total harmonic control!

(X = APPROACH NOTES)

That is just one example. What you will want to do—with EVERY chord progression you want to master melodically/harmonically in this wayis:

1. Identify the arpeggios of the chords in question and how long each chord lasts.
2. Break the arpeggios into usable melodic bits (with or without approach or connecting notes).
3. Practice switching between those bits at the points where the chords change.
4. Practice slowly at first, as slowly as you must to actually *think* about what you are doing.
5. Gradually build up speed and command.
6. Keep it interesting—flowing—and musical!

The Brecker Bros. sidemen in '85: me, Richie Morales, Mark Gray and Marcus Miller.

PART 2 The II-V Progression

You know, there are plenty of jazz books that write out some little II-V-I lick over and over again in each key, the same thing every time:

ETC. ETC. ETC.!!

Well, guess what? We are not going to do that here! Because what we are going for is complete *flexibility* and *multi-directionality* in our improvisations. The notes of every chord we will ever see are right there under our fingers, each arpeggio extending up and down, through the full range of our instrument! It is just up to us to know *what they are, what they sound like, and how to use them.* I have to say it again: *controlling the harmony melodically* - that is what this book is all about!

We are going to start here with the most basic kind of II-V progression - that is, a IIm7 going to an un-altered Vdom7. Let's stick with the concept of using mostly 4-note arpeggio fragments and play over some II-V's descending in whole steps.

I'm sure you noticed that we threw in a little chromaticism on the Bbm7-Eb7 near the end there! But we did make sure to put chord tones on the strong beats! That example was a sequence of descending II-V progressions in whole steps starting from Dm7... covering six keys. Say! I've got a great idea! Why don't we start from Ebm7, and do the other six?

That was nice. See how clearly the harmony comes out in the melodic line when we restrict ourselves to almost exclusively chord notes? And also how *close* all the arpeggios of the different chords are to each other? A note from one chord's arpeggio is never more than a whole step away from a note of the following chord. This convenient fact can be put to good use by the modern jazz soloist!

Now, before we move on, I would like YOU to try something: Look at the changes from one or both of the last two examples. Just one bar at a time if you have to. Play the arpeggios from each chord. Then, *slowly and carefully*, start assembling some II-V licks using 4-note bits from each changing arpeggio. Play a few on each II-V. Then, start moving through the keys. I think you will find it quite stimulating, rewarding - and also fun!

I think it would be a good idea to run our II-V progressions through some other sequences, don't you? We can play them ascending chromatically, as in parts of Coltrane's "Moment's Notice":

I am trying to get as much *melodic variety* (switching inversions, directional changes, etc.) as possible into these exercises, given the restrictions (almost all arpeggio notes) that we are making for ourselves here. But if you encounter a one-bar II-V phrase here that you particularly like, there is certainly no law against running it chromatically up and down your axe. In fact, I recommend it!

For instance, we could take the second bar of the previous example and repeat it like this:

(See following page)

● ●

As I said over and over again in *The Serious Jazz Practice Book*, it's all about getting as many note combinations as possible thoroughly learned and safely under your fingers. The difference is that here they are *harmonically based* note combinations. In the other book they were purely melodic. Both can be quite useful, however.... if I do say so myself!

Playing your II-V progressions *downward* chromatically is also a worthwhile thing to do. I'm sure you will agree!

There are a great variety of dom7 chord alterations that can be emphasized over the V chord in the II-V progression, which we will get into in MUCH more detail a little later. But for now, let's get our ears accustomed to the sounds of the various scales (diminished, altered, whole tone) that can lend some distinctive harmonic colors to the Vdom7 change. We can actually hear the tonalities more clearly if we make the chords one bar each instead of two beats. So let's do that!

SECTION II •

PART 3 The Minor II-V

The minor II-V is another of the most commonly seen progressions in jazz. It is a little different from the major II-V in that the II chord is *IIm7b5* instead of a straight IIm7 chord. This is because the chord built from the 7th degree of the diatonic scale (VIIm7b5) is actually the II chord of the 6th natural minor mode.

In fact, if we were to stay completely within the scale, the V chord in the minor II-V would be a minor 7th - actually the *phrygian* minor 7th built from the 3rd degree - but the V chord in a minor II-V is customarily some kind of dom7th chord. However, because the phrygian scale contains the degrees of b9, #9 (well, minor 3rd actually, but it becomes the #9 against a dom7th chord), and #5, the Vdom7th chord in a minor II-V is particularly compatible with those alterations - and therefore with the altered scale!

Of course, there is absolutely nothing wrong with playing a straight dom7th arpeggio as the V chord in the minor II-V (sequence here descending in whole steps again):

And let's play over the same chord pattern a half step up, just to cover all the keys:

But making use of the altered scale and accenting its various alterations (b5, #5, b9, #9) on the Vdom7th chord is the way to take maximum advantage of the minor II-V's tonal possibilities! We'll make the chords last one bar apiece again for this example. Here we will go with arpeggio notes on the IIm7b5 and altered scale variations on the Vdom7:

(See following page)

An interesting option to use on the minor II-V is to make the II chord a m7b5 with a *natural 9th* (also known as m9b5). In this example you can see how if we add the natural 9 (C#) to the Bm7b5 chord, the upper structure (without the B) becomes a Dm(maj7) chord. This takes the tonality of the Bm7b5 chord out of the C major scale and puts it into D melodic minor... in the 6th mode! (a.k.a. locrian ♮2). Still, there is only a one note difference – the C (from the C scale) becomes a C#!

So if we are going to play the minor II-V this way - as a 2m9b5 to a 5dom7(alt) - we had better be doing some serious wood-shedding on our melodic minor scales! Because we will be shifting them *up a minor third*, as in this example, from D melodic minor on the Bm9b5 to F melodic minor (E altered) on the E7alt chord.

The *natural 9 of the IIm9b5* resolving down to the *#5 of the Vdom7th* chord is a nice bit of voice movement to pay attention to here:

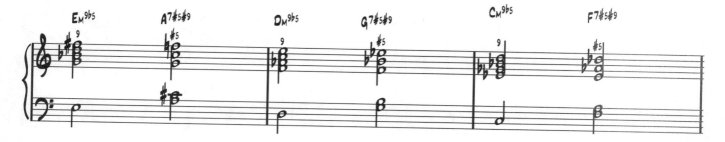

Japan 1985 - that's late great keyboard player Mark Gray, Lincoln Goines, Idris Muhammad, Sumo ozeki (champion) Kitao, Bob Mintzer, me, and two dudes whose names I can't remember!

If we accent those tones on the strong beats, we can melodically bring out their tonal colors:

(Remember, any one of these two-bar phrases can make a great bit to practice in all keys!)

And also notice that the top 3 notes of the m9b5 chord - the b5, b7, and 9 - make up an *augmented* triad. And if we move that augmented triad down a *half step*, we get the 1, 3, and #5 of the V chord. So we could choose to play nothing but augmented triads descending chromatically on this chord sequence, or we could choose on the V chord to play the *quartal triad* - containing the b7, #9, and #5 - that forms the top part of the dom7#5#9 voicing.

Of course, there are a lot more choices for triads of all kinds in the upper structure of the dom7 chord, as well as in many other chords. We will get to examine them momentarily. But first, let's take a look at probably the most important chord change of all!

PART 4 The Vdom7th Chord and the V-I Progression

a) The Basic Dom7th

Play a tritone. The harmonic tension contained in that little interval has dominated many a piece of music! (Could that be why they call it the dominant 7th chord?) In any case, the notes in the tritone can be either the 3rd or the 7th of two different Vdom7th chords (not coincidentally, a tritone apart), and they ache to resolve to their respective I chords... which can be either major or minor.

In fact, the two dom7th chords that contain any given tritone are so closely related harmonically that they can be substituted for each other in many situations. In this case the G7 could resolve down to F# and the C#7 could resolve to C - making it not a Vdom7-I but a *bIIdom7-I progression*... a phenomenon you have probably heard of, known as *tritone substitution*! But more on that later.

Notice that the 3rd of the V chord wants to resolve *up chromatically to the tonic of the I chord*, while the 7th wants to go *down*... either chromatically to the major 3rd of the I chord, or a whole step to the minor 3rd if it is a I minor chord. This is the primary voice movement in the progression.

So what does this mean melodically? Well, it means that the modern jazz soloist had better have a good command of his dominant 7th chord arpeggios, and be able to resolve them in any direction to his I chord of choice.

Now, let's get into that concept in a little more detail, shall we? Let's do V-I maj7 and V-I minor progressions descending in whole steps.

And let's take the same sequence up a half step - just to cover all the keys:

(continued on next page)

It sounds a little like J.S. Bach in places, doesn't it? That's because Bach was very fond of the Vdom7-I progression. He would use it to modulate all over the place! And Bach's music, to me, is kind of like the bebop of classical music! Check out his solo violin Sonatas and Partitas and you will see what I am talking about.

There are a lot of other ways to utilize the straight Vdom7 arpeggio. But I will leave it to you to find them! Practice breaking them up and turning them around, *in all keys*, and you will surely discover a wealth of melodic material.

But the most interesting thing about the V-I progression is the amazing number of variations and alterations that can be made on the Vdom7 chord, each one contributing its own distinct *sound* and *harmonic color* to the repertoire of the modern jazz soloist!

b) The 7b9 Chord

One of the coolest and amazingly versatile variations is the 7b9 chord, which is also known as the diminished 7th (each of the diminished chord's four possible roots can also be the b9 of four possible 7b9 chords). See in this example how when we drop any of the notes in the dim7 (7b9) chord one half step, it becomes a straight dom7 chord in the key of the dropped note!

And also notice how the diminished 7th chord contains *two tritones* - a minor 3rd apart - and that each one can be regarded as the 3rd and/or 7th of two different dom7 chords!

This means that we can use the same symmetrical diminished 7th arpeggio as a 7b9 variation on *four different Vdom7th chords*, and can resolve them to *any of their major or minor I chords* - a total of eight possible V-I resolutions from one arpeggio!

Of course, we will not want to just play the arpeggios up and down like in that example. We will want to use some scale bits (both diminished and diatonic) and approach notes to jazz it up a little! Let's try the other two dim7 arpeggios - as 7b9's - and resolve them to their possible I chords.

(continued on next page)

It kind of boggles the mind, doesn't it? There are just so many places these same arpeggios can resolve to! And if you treat them not as dom7b9 chords but as straight diminished 7th's, they can be used as passing chords to a lot of other places... almost anywhere, in fact! But we will get into some of that diminished chord stuff later. Right now we are on the subject of dom7th chords!

c) The Upper Extensions - 9th and 13th

Now we get into a very interesting area: the upper extensions of the dom7 chord. I am assuming that most of you already know that the upper extensions are built by adding thirds to the top of your 7th chords in whatever key you are in. If we are talking about the Vdom7 chord in the diatonic scale, we are in the mixolydian mode, so in the key of C, our thirds will go up from G, forming the upper extensions of the G7 chord:

If we were to build chords from each of those G7 chord degrees, they would look like this:

We can easily see that these are the diatonic 7th chords in the key of C. They are just in a different order, since they are being built up in thirds starting from G.

Now, first let us take a look at the first extension chord: Bm7b5. If we analyze it from G, it contains the 3, 5, b7, and 9... in other words, it is a G7(9) chord without the G! (If we analyze it from D, it is also a Dm6... containing the 1, b3, 5, and 6.)

In jazz, the bass player is usually playing the root (or 3rd or 5th) of the chord behind the soloist. Therefore, the greater our command of the upper extensions, the more melodic and harmonic color and variety we will be able to superimpose over those same bass notes!

Attaining mastery over the 7(9) chord - the m7b5 chord starting from the 3rd of the dom7th chord - is a great place to start the long process of getting control of *all* the possible extensions and alterations. Let's play some Vdom7(9) arpeggios resolving to Imaj7's... going up chromatically this time!

I encourage you (again!) to review the arpeggio exercises in *The Serious Jazz Practice Book*. Make up some studies, exercises, and licks of your own on each type of arpeggio. Then practice them through ALL the keys. For example, on this one, you might do something like this:

The next three chords built from the G7 chord notes - Dm7, Fmaj7, and Am7 - all contain the C, or 11th. So if we analyze them from the G they would all fall into the sus4 chord category - Dm7/G is G9(11), Fmaj7/G is G9(11/13), etc. And the Vdom7sus4 (or 11) chord is a harmonic substitute for the IIm7. It just has the 5th in the bass. So these chords, while very usable, would fall into the category of the II-V progressions we discussed earlier.

The true color of the 13th in the dom7 chord comes out when we drop the 4th (11th) down to the 3rd. Now, the Fmaj7 chord, built from the b7 of the G7 chord, contains - *against G* - the b7, 9, 11, and 13. So when we drop the C (the 11) in that chord down to B (the 3), we get a true G13 chord - containing the tritone foundation of the b7 and 3, and also the 9 and 13. But if you look at it by itself - without the G in the bass - *it is an Fmaj7b5 chord!*

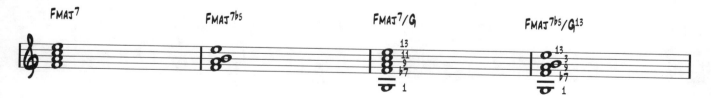

Now, this little arpeggio form (the maj7b5) has a multitude of uses and harmonic colors, depending on the bass note that accompanies it. But to really give that 13th chord sound against the dom7 chord, play it starting from the b7 - or a whole step down from your 7th chord! Here for your edification are a lovely bunch of Vdom7(13)-Imaj7 resolutions:

(See following page.)

ETC.

d) The Flipping the 13th chord to a 7(#5#9)

Once we have the maj7b5 arpeggios under our fingers, it's not that hard to *play* them. What *is* difficult is *thinking of them and using them as different chords*, over all the various bass notes that they can be played over! But with practice - a *lot* of practice - it becomes easier and more natural. Let's go over them in all the keys, just to prepare ourselves for what's coming up!

Notice the *third* chord possibility there. That's right, the chord we have been talking about, Fmaj7b5 (4 bars from the end), does not just double as G13, *it is also a Db7#5#9*! Yes, tritone substitution is kicking in here! The tritone notes (F and B) that were the b7 and 3 of the G7 chord simply flip to become the 3 and b7 over the Db. But at the same time, the A and E that were the 9 and 13 over the G now, in Db, become the #5 and #9 respectively! (Just for your information, this chord can also be a Dm6/9.)

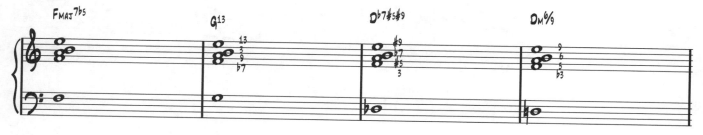

60

SECTION II ●

Now this is some very hip shit we are talking about here! But if, as we said, we have the basic materials under our fingers, it just becomes a matter of *being conscious of the possibilities* - and knowing how to use them! One thing to keep in mind is that using the Fmaj7b5 arpeggio as a Db7#5#9 will take its tonality out of C major (as in G mixolydian for the G13 chord) and into D melodic minor (Db altered).

So let's practice using our maj7b5 arpeggios as Vdom7#5#9's and resolving them to their respective I chords... major and minor!

(continued on next page)

61

The major resolution is OK, but I think the minor one is the more satisfying of the two. Why don't we take the Vdom7#5#9 - I minor through all the keys with a quicker one-bar resolution?

And while we are at it, let's do it in a circle of fourths pattern too! And don't forget - you can pick out any one of these two-bar bits and practice it all over your axe!

ETC.

e) The 7#11 Chord (including 9#11 and 13#11)

The dom7#11 chord is kind of unique in the family of dom7th chords. Unlike just about every other type of dom7th, including its very close relative, the straight dom7b5, *it is almost never used as a Vdom7 resolving to a I chord*. I say *almost* because there are always going to be exceptions. But much more often you will see the V chord's tritone substitute *bIIdom7#11* resolving to a Imaj7 or Im7. And frequently we see this type of 7th chord as either a IIdom7 or a IVdom7, relative to the key of the tune it appears in.

So why might that be? Jazz tradition, perhaps? I think that probably the reason is *common tones*. You will often hear the IIdom7#11 after a Imaj7 in a situation like this ("A Train" changes):

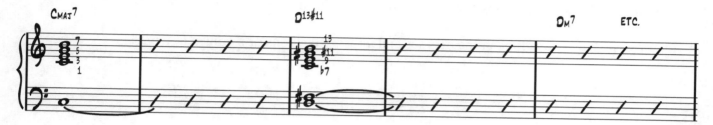

Here we can see that the notes in the Cmaj7 chord (1-3-5-7) barely change when they become the top part of the D13#11 (b7-9-#11-13). Only the G goes up to a G#!

You might also see the IVdom7#11 following the Imaj7 in this kind of context ("On A Clear Day"):

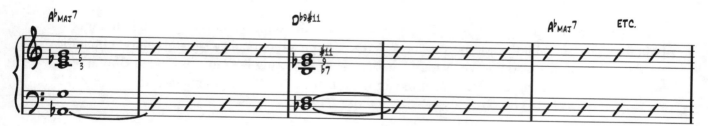

And there, similarly, only one note changes from the top three notes (3-5-7) in the Abmaj7 when they become the b7-9-#11 of the Db9#11 chord. The C goes down to a B!

And as we said, the bIIdom7#11 will resolve quite nicely to a Imaj7 or Im7. And we can see, just as in the previous examples, both of those cases have two common-tone holdovers, with only one note (albeit different ones) changing in the upper structure!

You might even see a *bVIIdom7#11*, where the top 3 notes of the bVII chord are the 1-3-5 major triad of the Imaj7 ("Killer Joe"):

But rarely will you hear a Vdom7#11 resolving to a I chord!

In any case, let's take a look at the degrees and upper extensions of a dom7#11 from C:

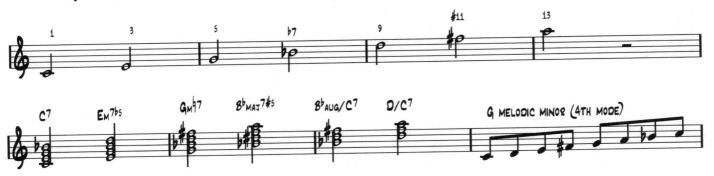

As you can see, the first two chords (C7 and Em7b5) are the same as they would be in the mixolydian mode. But then the addition of the #11 (the F#) puts the tonality squarely into G melodic minor (its 4th mode - also known as C lydian dominant), creating the Gm(maj7) and Bbmaj7#5 chords. Also notice that you can look at the upper structure as a Bb augmented triad (b7, 9, #11) or a D triad (9, #11, 13) over the lower structure of C7!

And it is the sound of that *major chord a whole step higher than the tonic* - in combination with the *augmented triad* starting from the b7th of the lower part - that gives the 7#11 chord its unique tonal quality!

So when soloing on the 7#11, we will want to emphasize the notes of those colorful upper arpeggios - either the minor(maj7) starting from the 5th of the chord, or the maj7#5 starting from the b7! Let's see if we can do that in a circle of fourths progression, which will take us through all the keys:

As we have seen, this chord form can appear in a lot of different places, so it's a good thing to have a strong *melodic command of its sound* under our fingers. And while we are at it, we may as well practice using it as a bIIdom7#11 resolving to either a I major7 or minor7!

(See following page)

f) 7b5 and 7#5 Chords

Now let's take a step backwards for a moment and look at two simpler dom7th chords which have only one alteration: a flatted or sharp 5th. The interesting thing about these chords is that their one single alteration can take them in several different directions, scale-wise. For instance, on the 7b5, the b5 alteration could be a passport into lydian dominant mode, as in the 7#11 chords we just discussed. Or it could just as easily serve as a point to take the chord's tonality into whole tone, diminished, or even altered! Play the arpeggio and pivot off the b5 into the various scales and you will see what I mean.

Similarly, the 7#5 chord can be played into either whole tone or altered scale mode.

The point of this is that when you see a 7b5 or 7#5 chord, you will have quite a few scale choices, so... use them wisely! But of course, it is never a bad idea to run through their basic arpeggios in all the keys. You can be sure that *those* notes will never be wrong when you see that chord symbol! First, let's do the 7b5's:

(See following page.)

Hey, wait a minute! We don't have to go through all 12 keys, we can stop there! Because - guess what? The notes of the C7b5 arpeggio are identical to those of the F#7b5, just like the F7b5 and the B7, etc. Every 7b5 chord has the exact same notes as the one a tritone away! Pretty neat, huh? It makes for a very clean and seamless tritone substitution in any case.

But let's not get sidetracked. I think we should play through the 7#5 arpeggios as well before we move on to the really heavy stuff!

PART 5 Triad Transformation

Obviously, there are quite a few other types of dom7th chords that we need to discuss here, which contain a lot of combinations of possible alterations in their upper extensions... b5's, #5's, b9's, #9's. Even a few 13's! Now, it is understood (I hope!) that all these alterations and extensions will be made over the basic *foundation notes* - root, 3rd, and b7th - of the dom7th chord.

Very interestingly, however, it so happens that certain *major, minor and also quartal and augmented triads - when superimposed over that foundation* - present a great way to state those alterations. We are familiar with these chords already; they are strong, basic harmonic forms. We just have to learn to use them in this different context!

a) Major Triads

First, let's analyze the major triads that can (and can't) be used as dom7th extensions. The ones that don't work against the dominant 7th can be handy too - but just in other situations! For example, look at the E/C (Cmaj7#5). A triad *a major 3rd above the root* is a wonderful thing to play against a maj7#5 chord... because it *makes* a maj7#5 chord! You can also always use the triad *a 5th above the root* as a replacement for Imaj7, as in the case of G/C (a Cmaj9 without the 3rd). And the triad which sits *a half step below the root* (such as B/C) is great against a diminished chord!

But back to the subject of dom7th chords!

We already have discussed the D major triad in the upper extensions of the C13#11 chord. But now look at these other triads. There is the Eb, *a minor 3rd above the root*, which makes a 7#9. The Gb, *a tritone away*, makes a 7b5b9. The Ab, *a minor 6th above the root (or a major 3rd down)*, makes a 7#5#9, and the A, *a minor 3rd below the root (or a major 6th up)* makes a 13b9 chord. I threw in the Bb here for good measure (a whole step down, of course), even though it really isn't a dom7th, but makes a sus chord with the b7, 9, and 11.

Notice that three of these triads - the Eb, Gb, and A - are part of the C half-step diminished scale (C would be the other triad in the sequence). So that scale could be used on any of those chords (built over the C7 foundation of course). The Ab/C7 forms a C7#5#9, so it would call exclusively for the C altered scale - which would also be a possibility on the Gb/C7 - the C7b5b9!

Remember: what we are talking about here is how to *control the harmony melodically*. There is a *big* difference between playing *over* these multi-tonal types of chords (when there is a chordal instrument playing behind you) and actually *stating (or implying)* those chords when you are playing with just a bass player, or by yourself!

The triads give us some neat little packages with combinations of *which alterations of the upper extensions* to accent. But this should always be done with an awareness of the underlying 7th chord! So if we can include some notes from that under-structure (such as the root, 3rd, and b7th), and combine them with the triads containing the altered notes, and do it in a soulful and musical way... well, then we will have something!

b) Minor Triads

Just a little more analysis, then we can get back to playing! There are several *minor* triads that can also be useful in the strange upper territories of altered dom7th chords. I don't think it's necessary to list all the ones that don't really work this time. Let's just look at these:

The most common would probably be the minor triad a half step above the root, Dbm/C7. This is not surprising, since the C7 altered scale is, of course, Db melodic minor! This chord becomes a C7#5b9. Then we have the Ebm/C7, which switches those alterations, making a *C7b5#9*! Either the altered or the diminished scale could apply on that one.

(See following page)

The F#m/C7 is a diminished scale-based chord that can be analyzed as a C13b5b9. But this is the type of chord I like to call a diminished (double extended) because the top two notes are extended one scale step from a dim7th chord (there is a lot more on this in *The Serious Jazz Practice Book*). You could play around using only the notes from the F#m triad and C7 understructure, but you might have more fun just playing the dim(extended) chords up in minor 3rds!

The Gm/C7 kind of speaks for itself - it is just a straight C7(9) chord (without the 3rd). It is a good idea to remember, however, that the triads containing the normal, conventional sounding upper extensions are right there next to the more bizarre and adventurous altered ones!

And the Bbm/C - also sometimes known as 7b9sus - is useful in another way. It serves as a substitute for a m7b5 chord, but with the 5th in the bass (the notes of Bbm are the top three notes of Gm7b5). So we might play the Bbm arpeggio before resolving it to one of our altered C7 chords in a minor II-V-I progression.

c) Quartal Triads

Quartal triads are also handy little devices that can fit into a LOT of places, harmonically speaking. Especially the perfect 4th ones! Just take a look at them here against C and think about what they become and how we might be able to use them:

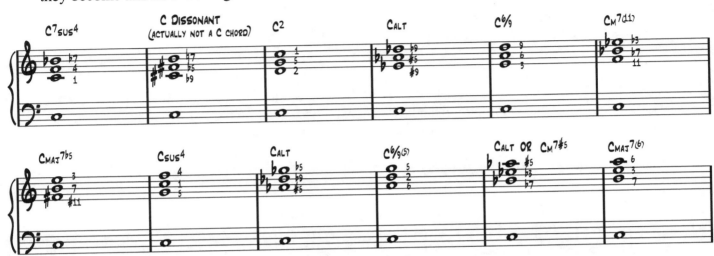

Now since we are on the subject of altered dom7th chords, I direct your attention to the three "Calt" choices. The first one (4th chord above, line 1) contains the #9, #5 and b9. The second (3rd chord above, line 2) has the #5, b9 and b5, and the third one (second from the end) the b7, b3 (#9) and #5.

So any one of these could be a good choice to accent *those particular alterations* on a dom7th chord. And their nice "fourthy" quality makes a pleasant contrast to the 3 and b7 of the dom7th!

Of course, I am sure you can see how the quartal triads can be used in lots of other places as well, against a great variety of major, minor, sus4, and even regular non-altered dom7th chords (the 1-5-2 and 6/9 varieties are a good choice for the latter). Practice them in all the keys, they will serve you well!

The other quartal triads - that contain a tritone - can also be useful as upper alterations of the dom7th (and other chords), usually in a diminished scale context. Some of these contain combinations of the 5 and b5! The ones from the half-step diminished scale are the ones that would go over the dom7th:

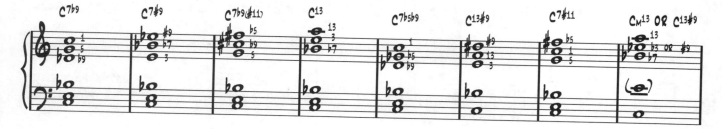

These babies can be played either as single arpeggios or as patterns in minor 3rds:

And then there are the ones from the regular (whole-step) diminished scale. It is tempting to think of these as lydian chords - maj7b5 chords without the 3rd - and they could be used that way over those bass notes, but we need to look at them in the diminished scale context:

And actually I think it is better to practice them purely as diminished patterns. And mix 'em up!

d) Augmented Triads

It is also a very good thing to always be aware of the augmented triads and their roles in the various types of dom7th chords. The one containing the root, 3rd and #5 can be viewed as part of either the whole tone or *altered scale* and can be played nicely over any 7th chord containing a #5. The one a whole step up (or a whole step down!) contains the b7, 9 and #11 (perfect over those #11 chords!) and therefore would be part of the *lydian dominant scale* as well as whole tone. Interestingly, the altered scale and the lydian dominant scale are both modes of the melodic minor scale, and over any given bass note, the two melodic minor scales used to make those modes will be a tritone apart!

Since every augmented triad has three possible roots, it stands to reason that each one can substitute for three different dom7#5 chords! Which could resolve to their respective minor I's as in this example:

Or they could be the b7-9-#11 of three different 9(#11) chords, which could resolve a half step down to their maj7 chords in a series of bIIdom9(#11)-Imaj7 progressions:

Yes, those augmented triads are some versatile little suckers, aren't they? One more thing: playing them up in half steps (or down in minor thirds) will create a nifty pattern that can go over 7th chords either in a circle of fourths or descending chromatically:

Triad Reference Guide

I made the following little reference guide just to keep all the triads and their relationships to all the possible bass notes absolutely mind-bogglingly clear! This describes what chords are formed when triads move up (or down) in relation to a stationary bass note. All chords are I chords unless otherwise noted.

MAJOR TRIAD	CREATES:
On root	major chord
half step up	bIImaj7 chord with 7th in the bass
whole step up	maj6/9(#11), dom13#11 or a IIdom7 with the b7 in the bass
minor 3rd up	m7 or dom7#9
major 3rd up	maj7#5
fourth up	IV major triad with the 5th in the bass
tritone up	#IV/I polychord or a dom7b5b9
fifth up	major9 chord with no 3rd
flat 6th up	dom7#5#9 or a bVI triad with the 3rd in the bass
minor 3rd down	dom13b9
whole step down	dom7(9-11) or minor7(9-11)
half step down	diminished(extended)

MINOR TRIAD	CREATES:
On root	minor chord
half step up	dom7#5b9
whole step up	IVmajor 6th chord with the 5th in the bass, or IIm7 with the 7th in the bass
minor 3rd up	m7b5 or dom7b5#9
major 3rd up	maj7
fourth up	IV minor triad with the 5th in the bass
tritone up	dom13b5b9
fifth up	dom7(9) with no 3rd
flat 6th up	bVIm/I polychord (diminished double extended)

(continued on next page)

minor 3rd down	I major 6th or VI minor triad with the 3rd in the bass
whole step down	7(b9)sus
half step down	maj7(9-#11)

QUARTAL TRIAD (perfect 4th)   CREATES:

On root	7sus4
half step up	nothing! (except maybe a passing chord)
whole step up	maj(2)chord (containing the 1, 2, and 5)
minor 3rd up	7th chord alterations #9, #5, and b9
major 3rd up	maj6/9 (with 3rd)
fourth up	m7(11)
tritone up	maj7b5
fifth up	sus4
flat 6th up	7th chord alterations #5, b9, and b5
minor 3rd down	6/9 with 5th (can be major or minor)
whole step down	m7#5 (or b7-#9-#5 of dom7th)
half step down	maj7(6)

QUARTAL TRIADS (tritone-perfect 4th)   CREATES:

On root	maj7b5 (no 3rd)
half step up	b9, 5 and 1 - could be bIImaj7b5/I or part of 7b9
whole step up	nothing! (except maybe a passing chord)
minor 3rd up	minor6/9
major 3rd up	7#9
fourth up	IVmaj7#11 with 5th in bass (lydian modal chord)
tritone up	#IVmaj7b5 with b5 in bass
fifth up	5, b9, b5 (a half-step diminished-based dom 7th)
flat 6th up	IVminor 6/9 with 5th in bass - or bVImaj7b5 with 3rd in bass
minor 3rd down	diminished(extended)

whole step down	dom7(13)
half step down	nothing! (except maybe a Vdom7#9/I)

QUARTAL TRIADS
(perfect 4th-tritone)

CREATES:

On root	IVmaj7#11(no 3rd)/I or IIminor13 with 7th in bass
half step up	b9, b5 and 1 - could be upper part of 7b9b5
whole step up	nothing! (except maybe a passing chord)
minor 3rd up	IVminor13/I
major 3rd up	13#9
fourth up	dom7sus(3 added)
tritone up	diminished(double extended)
fifth up	5, 1, b5 (another half-step diminished-based dom 7th)
flat 6th up	bII lydian with maj7 in bass or bVII minor13/I
minor 3rd down	I have no idea!
whole step down	minor13
half step down	maj7 with a b7 on top??

AUGMENTED TRIADS

On root	augmented triad - could be part of dom7#5 or maj7#5
half step up	bIImaj7#5 chord with the 7th in the bass or bVIIm9(maj7)
whole step up	dom9#11
minor 3rd up	minor(maj7)

It's true, you can go crazy trying to analyze some of these! The important thing is to be aware of all the possibilities that spring from these chords... what scales they can be part of, how we can use them to inspire our melodic creativity, and ultimately - how we put it all together!

PART 6 Diminished Chords

Well, there is just one more type of chord form to go over here, and that would be the diminished chord. We have already discussed the dim7th arpeggios - when used as Vdom7b9's - resolving to any of four possible I major or I minor chords, and the quartal triads (containing tritones) that can be used in the diminished chord category as well as dom7.

I want to remind everyone that there are about 50 pages of diminished scale-based stuff in *The Serious Jazz Practice Book* and there are *tons* more just waiting to be discovered and practiced by you!

But the important thing to keep in mind about the diminished 7th arpeggio is that it can serve as a passing chord - a set of passing notes - to almost anywhere... to any other chord. You will hear a lot of straight diminished chord arpeggios in swing era type jazz. For instance, Django Reinhardt or Johnny Hodges might have played something like this, with a Idim7 going back and forth to a I major chord:

You might also see a diminished passing chord (or arpeggio) connecting any of the diatonic 7th chords. Some of these, of course, could be seen as Vdom7b9's resolving to their respective I's:

But since we have already gone over the dom7b9 aspect of the dim7 chord, the other most useful way to play the dim7 arpeggio is simply as a Idim7 to a I major or minor chord. Of course, there are four of each, for each dim7 chord! We'll do the majors first:

(continued on next page)

And then the minors:

SECTION III PLAYING ON TUNES (The Harmonic Approach)

OK. So here we are, armed with our knowledge of all the different chord forms, scales, arpeggios, upper extensions, alterations, approach notes, harmonic regions, strong beats, etc. etc. etc!!

How - you might well ask - can we actually *apply* all of this to the basic, fundamental task we all have as jazz musicians... which is to create good, musical solos? How can all this *information* actually *improve our improvisation*?

The key is CHOICES. We now have at our disposal a LOT of choices which can enable our creativity to take flight in a very intelligent and musical way! We just need to be aware of the best ways, and also the best *places*, musically speaking, to *use* what we have learned.

When do we stay completely within the basic chord? When do we use the upper extensions? Under what circumstances do we use the various alterations? Substitutions? Scale choices? Chromatic passing bits?

Some of this is obviously going to be left to the aesthetic taste of the individual improvisor, because there are so many ways to use these materials and so many different styles of playing.

But there *are* some overall principles which apply. And I think a very good way to get into them gradually is to take a look at the various harmonic possibilities that can arise from that most basic vehicle for the jazz soloist: the blues!

PART 1 Expanding the Blues

Let's start right at the beginning and make a little melody on this all-time classic form: a 3-chord, 12-bar blues in Bb! Since I just wrote it, I believe I will call this one "Barry's Blues".

BARRY'S BLUES

83

Now, of course we could solo over this tune using nothing but the Bb minor pentatonic or the blues scale (adding the major 3rd and b5) and it would sound just fine. But since we are going to employ the *harmonic approach*, let's begin by making our note choices from the arpeggios of the three dom7th chords... with a few scale and approach notes thrown in. (I have to put in the grace notes too, for the sake of soulfulness!)

OK. So those three 7th chords are the most basic harmony we can use on the blues. But they can be *expanded upon and substituted for* in a great variety of ways! And if we can improvise - with *taste and soul* - while *melodically stating* those *alternate harmonies*, we will be greatly increasing our bluesy options!

One choice that comes to mind right away is to use the *upper extensions* of those 7th chords by playing Dm7b5 (Bb9) and/or Abmaj7b5 (Bb13) against the Bb7, and use the same relationships against the Eb7 (Gm7b5, Dbmaj7b5) and F7 (Am7b5, Ebmaj7b5).

Another thing we can easily do is to make those 7th chords into the V chords in II-V progressions... so the Bb7 would become Fm7-Bb7; the Eb7, Bbm7-Eb7; and the F7, Cm7-F7. This gives us a modal type of blues sound reminiscent of late 50's jazz.

Or we could treat the Bb and Eb as 13#11 chords (calling for the lydian dominant mode) and the F either as a straight 7b5 (whole tone) or as 7#5 (altered). And for good measure, let's throw in a Bb7#5#9 in the 4th bar. This creates a nice tension before resolving to the Eb chord!

These *tension areas* - which usually occur where a Vdom7 chord (or its tritone substitute, bIIdom7) is resolving to its relative I chord - are the places where *we can be the most creative* in terms of what kind of *harmonic colors* we put in our melodic lines by choosing from the many various alterations and scale choices that are available. The most obvious places for this in the 12-bar blues are the 4th bar, where the Bb7 goes to the Eb7, and the last bar, where the F7 goes back to the Bb. Which is what we just did!

But we can easily put some more tension areas in there! We can put a Bb7 altered chord on the last two beats of bar 1, going to the Eb. Then we can put an Edim7 passing chord on the second half of bar 2, which creates some nice tension leading back to the Bb7. (We can also do that at bar 10.) At bar 6, we can substitute Edim7 (remember, it is also an Eb7b9!) for the whole bar of Eb7.

And I suggest we keep the Bb and F altered 7th chords we already have at bars 4 and 12!

And remember, these are still just variations on a 3-chord blues. If we are going to be playing the "jazz blues" it will certainly contain a lot more changes than that! With lots more tension areas to sink our teeth into! In this key, we would still have the Bb7 altered chord (or an Fm7-Bb7 II-V) at bar 4. At bar 8, there will probably be a whole bar of G7 (or Dm7-G7), the VI dom7 chord resolving to the II chord in bar 9. And the last 4 bars of our jazz blues are usually 1 bar each of II and Vdom7 and then a *turnaround* - two beats each of either III-VI-II-V or I-VI-II-V.

There can be many variations on this general framework. The II chord in bar 9 can be either minor7 or dom7. The turnarounds can be IIIm7-VIdom7-IIm7-Vdom7, or they can *all* be dom7. If the I chord starts the turnaround, it can be dom7 or major7. If we use *tritone substitution* in the turnarounds we get some other interesting variations such as III-bIII-II-bII, III-bIII-bVI-bII, I-bIII-bVI-bII, bVII-VI-bVI-V, etc.

(See following page)

Yes, those turnarounds are places where we have a lot of harmonic choices that have to be made... *fast!* We should definitely plan to have plenty of them in our musical vocabulary! And if we start applying *tritone substitution* in the other tension areas of the form, bar 4 could be played as E7 (or Bm7-E7), bar 8 could be Db7 or Abm7-Db7, and bar 10 could be B7 or F#m7-B7!

It is interesting to note that if we substitute, for example, E7#11 for the Bb7altered in bar 4, the parent scale for both E lydian dominant and Bb altered - B melodic minor - *stays the same!*

There can be a lot more harmonic variations within the 12-bar jazz-blues form. The main thing to remember - when using the *harmonic approach* - is to *state that harmony* in our solos! It might be a blues that is packed with II-V progressions as in the changes of Charlie Parker's "Blues For Alice":

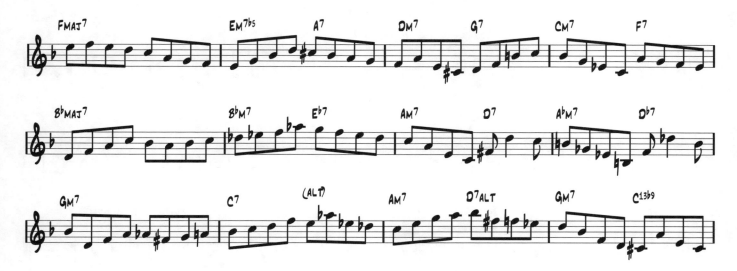

Or we could find ourselves playing on the changes of John Coltrane's "Some Other Blues", which has a nice circle of fourths cycle in the middle of it that we can choose to repeat (2 beats each) in the turnaround:

SECTION III • • • • • • • • • • • • • • • • • • •

PART 2 Minor Blues

Another blues form we will find ourselves soloing on very often is the minor blues. Typically in its most basic configuration we will see a harmonic pattern something like the one in this brand new spontaneously created composition by yours truly:

BARRY'S MINOR BLUES

B. FINNERTY

Now, of course we could just play C minor pentatonic over this whole thing. Or we could take a modal approach, going with C and F dorian on the minor 7th chords and Ab mixolydian and G7 altered on those respective 7th chords.

But again, there are plenty of places to add and superimpose those nice tension areas in the minor blues progression. Usually they will be altered 7th chords (or minor II-V's) resolving to their respective minor I chords. For example, we can put a G7 altered (or Db7#11 - or a minor II-V) at bar 2 - and also at bar 6 - to get us back to our tonic Cm7. At bar 4, we can change the Cm7 to a C7 altered going to the Fm7. And at bar 8, we can put an Eb7 (or Bbm7-Eb7) to get us to the Ab7 chord! (That's the one choice here that is not a minor II-V.)

(See following page.)

We can also add some tasty turnaround variations on the minor blues, most of which are pretty similar to the ones found in the standard blues.

PART 3 Rhythm Changes

Now, while we are on the subject of turnarounds, I think it would be a good idea to take a look at another one of the true classics among jazz improvisation forms: rhythm changes. When George Gershwin composed "I Got Rhythm" (with lyrics by his brother Ira) for the 1930 musical "Girl Crazy", I am sure he never imagined that this particular harmonic structure would become the basis for such an incredible number of jazz tunes!

But there are reasons why this tried and true set of chord changes has stood the test of time. For one thing, it is made up almost entirely of turnarounds! The main "A" section has them in bars 1-2, 3-4, and 7-8 (either I-VI-II-V or III-VI-II-V) and bars 5-6 could be looked at as a turnaround *to* the turnaround - containing Imaj-Idom7-IVmaj-IVm7 - before going back to the III-VI-II-V in bars 7-8. And the bridge is really one *long* turnaround - two bars each of III-VI-II-V - all of them dom7 chords!

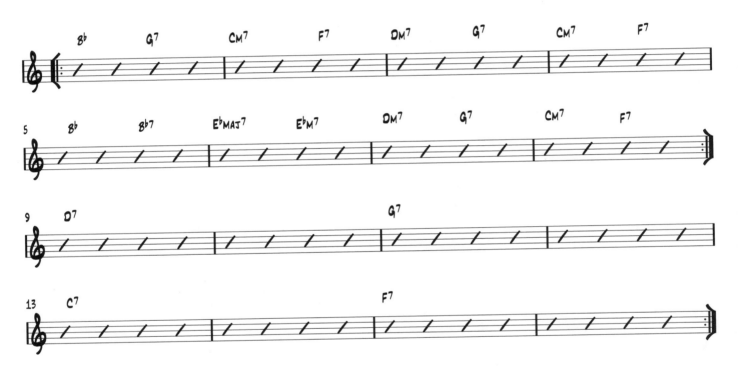

This opens up the chord sequences of rhythm changes into all the possible variations we examined earlier in the turnarounds at the end of the blues form... except in this case they are happening all the way through the tune! Any of the dom7 chords in the (2-bar) turnarounds can be replaced by their tritone substitutes, which can give us the combinations such as III-bIII-II-bII, III-bIII-bVI-bII, I-bIII-bVI-bII, bVII-VI-bVI-V, etc. And in the bridge, not only can each 7th chord be made into a II-V, it can also change into its tritone substitute - or *its* related II-V!

(See following page.)

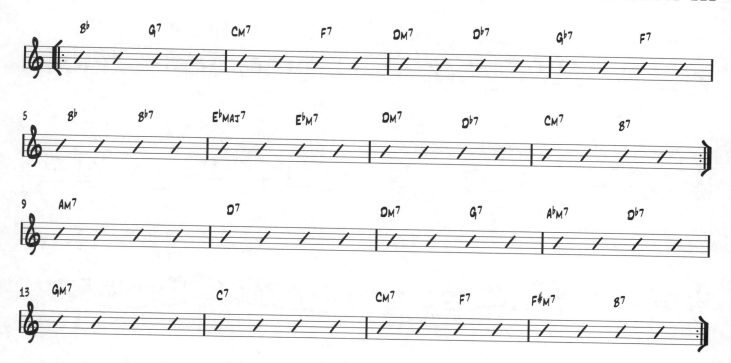

So what does this mean melodically? Well, it means that we had better be harmonically on our toes! Those changes in the "A" section are moving fast - and there are a ton of possible chord alterations and scale choices (again, particularly in those tension areas where the dom7 chords fall) that we can throw in to give color and creativity to our improvisations. (See following page.)

Montreux, 2004: I was fortunate to be able to jam with B.B. King after his main show on the big stage. This shot was from the video. He looks like he must have dug something I played! You can see the entire clip by searching for Barry Finnerty & B.B. King on YouTube.

There are just *so* many ways to go about this! As long as we make sure to pay particular attention to the strong beats where the alterations will be most clearly accented, we can use a great assortment of arpeggios and scales... even the chromatic scale!

And on each of the four 7th chords of the bridge, we have our choice of all the possible dom7 chord scales - diminished, whole tone, altered, etc. - not to mention our standard mixolydian (if we treat the chord as a II-V) and its tritone substitute!

And not necessarily in that order! In any case, rhythm changes are one of the staples of the jazz musician's repertoire, and I strongly urge you to practice them strenuously... in as many keys as possible!

SECTION III ●

PART 4 Coltrane's Changes: Giant Steps and Countdown

Most of you are probably already familiar with these tunes from John Coltrane's famous "Giant Steps" album—which was released in 1959—and contained some innovative harmonic sequences for soloing that jazz players have been grappling with ever since!

These chord changes require a lot of practicing - needless to say - to master. But the same principles that we have already discussed apply to them as well. We can use melodic variations on the exact arpeggios for each chord (which is the best way to make sure the harmony is *absolutely clearly stated* in our solos) as in this example on 16 bars of "Giant Steps":

Or we can use our various scale options, while making *sure* to place a chord tone—or if need be, a color tone that *resolves* to a chord tone—on every strong beat:

(continued on next page)

The same is true for the slightly more complicated "Countdown" changes. "Countdown" was actually written by extending the changes of an older tune, "Tune Up", which was made up mostly of II-V-I progressions. Mr. Coltrane took each 4-bar II-V-I sequence and changed it from this:

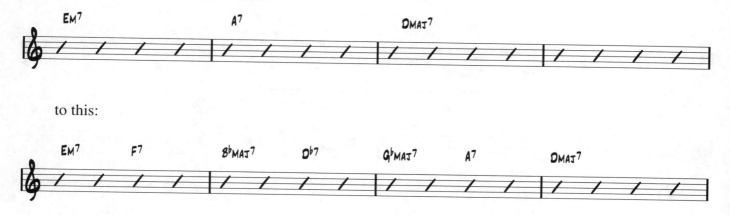

to this:

It's like taking the long way around that II-V! By adding two Vdom7-Imaj7 progressions in the middle of the sequence, Coltrane allows us to play in three keys instead of one during those 4 bars!

In keeping with the jazz tradition of writing songs based on the chord changes of another more famous song, I wrote a tune based on the changes to "Countdown" and called it... "Count Up"! It's on my "Straight Ahead" CD (Arabesque, '96) if anyone is interested... and is also presented here!

(see following page)

COUNT UP

- B. Finnerty

These changes are fun - and challenging - because we have to play through Coltrane's extended II-V-I changes in three different keys before getting to relax on one chord change per bar in the final four:

(continued on next page)

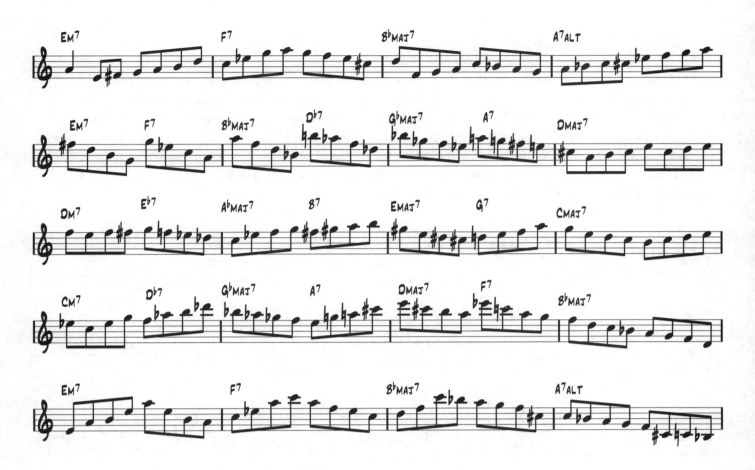

This shot is from Germany in '96 or '97 - we were playing the Frankfurt Music Messe – the world's biggest music fair – with organist Jon Hammond. That's my engineer, Joe Berger, also playing guitar in the lower left corner.

PART 5 Other Tunes

Of course, there are plenty of other well-known jazz tunes with chord changes that present interesting challenges to keep us on our toes, melodically and harmonically speaking! Many contain variations on the II-V-I and Vdom7 (or bIIdom7#11)-1 packages. Sonny Rollins' "Airegin" is a good example. Here the A section switches between Fm7 and F#dom7#11 (F minor to the F# lydian dominant or C7 altered mode of C# melodic minor) to the same kind of Vdom7alt/bIIdom7#11-Im7 movement in Bbm7; then the B section cycles through a bunch of II-V-I 's. It is important to keep aware of the strong beats and the voice movement we want to accent here:

(continued on next page)

Another interesting tune is Dizzy Gillespie's "Con Alma". In the A section of this tune the lead note G# changes its function - and *harmonic color* - four times, going from the 3rd of Emaj7 to the tonic of G#7, the 5th of C#m7, and the 7th of Bb7. This is a good example of what we discussed in Section One - how one note can spin off in a lot of different directions, as part of a great variety of scales and arpeggios:

A good rule of thumb to keep in mind while utilizing the *harmonic approach* is this: *the more complicated the changes, the more important it is to stay melodically within that harmony!*

In this example that was featured in *The Serious Jazz Practice Book*, we can see how with a little bit of motivic development we can make a very workable solo on Joe Henderson's rather harmonically advanced tune "Inner Urge" using *all* arpeggio notes:

Sometimes a tune will have common chord sequences mixed together with unconventional ones. The title tune of my most recently recorded CD "Clarita" is a good example of this:

(See following page)

CLARITA

For the solo section (which is kind of an extended variation of the changes on the melody - like my grandfather used to say, "the same thing, only different!") I wrote mostly II-V changes - either straight IIm7-Vdom7 or IIm7b5-Vdom7alt - but as you can see I threw in a few curveballs there! The 3rd bar is a II-V in the bass - but the V change is a maj7b5! And in the 6th bar the harmony is Fmaj7b5 going to F#maj7#5! Chord changes like that pretty much *require* that for those bars we need to draw our melodic figures from the most basic source - *the actual arpeggios of the chords in question* - before reverting (if we so choose) to more scale-based melodies on the regular II-V changes.

Then, on the bridge, we have three Vdom7alt-Im7 sequences before the Bb9#11-G9#11 change, which again compels us to really be *inside* those chords, particularly their upper extensions! Then after the Amaj7b5, we are back to a more conventional set of chords:

Let me try to sum this whole thing up! Obviously there are all kinds of tunes, containing all kinds of chord changes (not to mention melodies, rhythms, and structures). Probably 90% of them will fit into an easily identifiable category, i.e. pop, bop, jazz, standards, blues, fusion, Latin, Brazilian, etc. And most of them will contain some of the commonly used chord sequences we have worked on here, such as II-V's, III-VI-II-V's, Vdom7-I's, etc. But *every type of chord in every tune you will ever see* will be one of the chords we have discussed, analyzed, arpeggiated, and scaled here! It does not matter how unorthodox the *combinations* or *sequences* of chords in any particular tune might be. Some might very well be difficult to play on. But practice - sometimes *lots* of practice - will enable us to put it all together!

So, as I said in the Introduction (but I'm going to say it one more time!), as long as we thoroughly know the *exact notes* (and related scales) of *every chord we see* as jazz improvisors, we will have the most solid possible foundation to create spontaneous melodies that are infused with true clarity and musicality! That is the Harmonic Approach!

And now it is time to work on our....

July 2007: Me and Clarita at the 40th anniversary of the original Human Be-In in Golden Gate Park, San Francisco. Peace and love, baby!

SECTION IV HARMONIC VOCABULARY

I am going to assume that almost all of you, my dear readers, know your basic arpeggios by now and can play them in all the keys. If you need to refresh your memory, there is a very good section on all the most important ones and fun things to do with them in *The Serious Jazz Practice Book*. We are going to deal mostly with *combinations* of different arpeggios—naturally—because changing chords is what harmony is all about!

But just to get warmed up, let's start with a few basic arpeggio studies that we can repeat until they are comfortable under our fingers. These - like the exercises in *The Serious Jazz Practice Book* - are presented in one key only and should definitely be cycled through all the keys, and throughout the range of your instrument!

PART 1 Some Major Stuff

You know, it is really quite amazing what you can do with just the simple old major triad. It is such a strong and basic chord form - and therefore combinations of it can be very effective melodically in a lot of different contexts.

One of my personal favorites is to alternate between two major triads a whole step apart. This can be used nicely in mixolydian mode (and also in other modes such as phrygian, lydian or dorian):

And since the melodic minor scale also contains two major triads a whole step apart - built from its 4th and 5th degrees - we can also use those same two triads against the dom7#11 and (especially!) the altered 7th chords built from that melodic minor scale!

I don't think we need to write out this example - major triads a whole step apart - in every possible key. We know what they are now. We can go ahead and practice them! But here are just a few little suggestions of ways to do that:

(See following page)

Major triads going up in whole steps can also be a substitute for Vdom7(sus)-Imaj7 changes. In this example the notes of the C triad are the b7-9-11 in the first chord C/D, and when it moves up to D/G in the second chord, the degrees of *that* triad (over G) become 5-7-9 (a maj9 with no 3rd)! Then we repeat the sequence going down in whole steps.

When we play major triads and move them around in minor 3rds—or tritones—we get into some serious diminished scale territory. Again, there is a bunch of stuff on this in *The Serious Jazz Practice Book*. So, if you haven't got it yet, treat yourself, and go buy it already! But here are a few things we can throw in when we see those dom13b9 and 13#9 chords!

And very interestingly, if we move our major triads *down* in *major* 3rds, it can be a neat substitute for II-V changes! Here in the first II-V the C triad is the b3-5-b7 of Am7 (or, again, the b7-9-11 of a D7sus chord), and when it moves down a major 3rd the resulting Ab triad is the b5-7-b9 of the V chord, which here becomes a D7b5b9! We can continue this down chromatically or any way we like.

(See following page)

Now let's go from the ultra-hip to the ultra-simple! To state something I think should be obvious to everyone, major triads do not always have to be upper extensions of other chords. Sometimes - *most* of the time, actually - they are just major triads, and they carry their *own harmony* with them. So just the act of playing them - *in any order* - will immediately create and define that harmonic structure! And a LOT of tunes - though not always jazz tunes - are built entirely of simple, un-altered major chords! Why not take the all-time classic I-IV-V progression and make a little tune?

Barry's Calypso

B. Finnerty

OK, so I threw in a little I-VI-II-V there at the end! But we can see that playing those major triads through the circle of 4ths can give our melodies some real harmonic direction! Let's try doing that through all the keys and see what we can come up with:

(See following page)

Major Triads - circle of 4ths

We can also add a scale degree or passing tone in the middle of the triad to add a little melodic variety:

Major Triads - circle of 4ths w/passing tones

And it would not be a bad idea to run some *down* in 4ths and/or *up* in fifths! Don't you agree?

Major Triads - up in 5ths/down in 4ths

(continued on next page)

Or we could take one bar of that last sequence and repeat it down in whole steps:

Major Triads - in 5ths & minor 3rds

And one more very effective way to use major triads in a jazz context is to play them as *substitute turnaround* changes. We touched on this briefly in the previous section, but I would like to emphasize again that major chords over a I-bIII-bVI-bII progression provide a colorful and rock-solid alternative to the standard I(or III)-VI-II-V turnaround changes. I think this particular idea is important enough that we should run a few variations in almost all the keys:

Major Triad - 1-bIII-bVI-bII turnarounds

PART 2 Some Minor Stuff

You don't often see combinations of minor triads used in the same ways as the major triads in the previous examples. But it is still a good idea to practice playing them with all their possible passing tones and approach notes. Here are a few examples:

(continued on next page)

And as we discussed in detail in Section II, some of the most interesting ways to use basic harmonic materials such as minor (also major, augmented, and quartal) triads are as *upper extensions* of other chords that they can be part of. The 1, b3, and 5 of any minor triad can also be seen as the b3, b5, and b7 of the m7b5 chord starting a minor 3rd below our original minor triad. So for example, we can use them and drop one note to resolve to a dom7b9:

And if we move that triad containing the b3, b5, and b7 of the (II)m7b5 chord *up a minor third*, that minor triad becomes the b9, 3, and #5 of the (V)altered dom7th chord that the IIm7b5 is resolving to! This makes it a worthwhile thing to practice our minor triads in sequences going up in minor thirds, just so we can use them in those types of situations.

PART 3 Some Augmented Stuff

One of the cool things about the augmented triad is that depending on the bass note (from that triad's whole tone scale) being played underneath, each one can be the b7, 9 and #11 of three different dom9#11 chords, or the 1, 3 and #5 of three different dom7#5 chords. So each triad can serve as six dom7 chords from each scale. That's a lot of dom7 chords!

In the above example, of course, if each line were a whole step up (starting from D7#5 and Eb7#5), *the exact same relationships would apply.*

So whenever we see dom7 chords in a circle of 4ths - or descending chromatically (a tritone substitution for the same thing) - we can play augmented triads moving upwards chromatically:

Or we can play them going downwards in minor 3rds - which is an inversion of the previous idea:

Or downwards or upwards in 4ths or 5ths – *any* combination that switches between triads from the two whole tone scales will work against our dom7 circle of 4ths changes! In fact, try starting the circle of 4ths progression here with *any* of the six dom7 chords from the C whole tone scale:

So what I am saying is: practice those augmented arpeggios! They will serve you well.

PART 4 Tons of II-Vs!

We have already done our analysis of this most basic of jazz progressions. Our only remaining task here is to get as many variations under our fingers as possible. And there are plenty of them! I am going to write these out chromatically so as to cover all the keys. A special note to string players: try to play these in a lot of different positions!

Chromatic II-Vs

Chromatic II-Vs

Clearly, there are a LOT more variations on even the most basic II-V licks. But I have a good idea. Why don't we mix 'em up a little bit?

Chromatic II-Vs

And there is no reason why we can't play them *up* chromatically as well... is there?

Chromatic II-Vs (ascending)

II-V phrases can be fun when we use chromatic and/or diatonic passing tones to the chord tones on the strong beats:

Chromatic II-Vs w/passing tones

Or we can go even more chromatic - again, as long as we keep accenting those chord tones on the strong beats!

Chromatic II-Vs w/chromatic connections

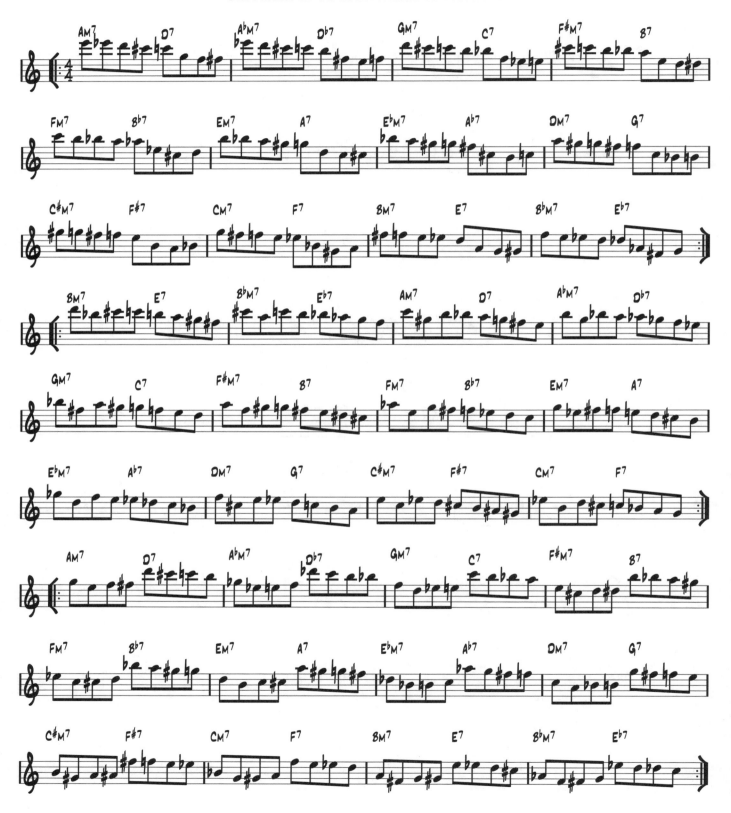

Then of course there are *all* the possible variations of *scales, alterations*, and also *chord substitutions* on that big tension area of the V chord! There are so many of these that it really does boggle the brain!

Let's look at some of the scale variations first, while stretching the changes out to one bar apiece so that we can clearly hear the difference in tonalities. We can go with (half-step) diminished on the V:

IIm7-Vdom7 *(half-step diminished)*

And why don't we kind of reverse that last one?

(See following page)

IIm7-Vdom7 (half-step diminished)

The altered scale is very similar to the half-step diminished - identical for the first 5 notes. But then it features its signature tone – *the #5* – where in the diminished scale we have the *natural 5 and 6*. Let's accent that distinctive note – the #5 – on the first strong beat of the Vdom7(alt) change here:

IIm7-Vdom7 (altered)

(continued on next page)

Or we can accent the tension of the downward motion from the 9th of the IIm7 chord to the #5 of the V chord on the first and second beats of the Vdom7 bar. And mix it up some more!

IIm7-Vdom7 (altered)

And, of course, it is always an option to go with the whole tone scale on the V chord, which can imply 7b5 or 7#5, depending on which note(s) we choose to accent:

IIm7-Vdom7b5 or #5 (whole tone)

But let's leave these scales for now and get back to those arpeggios! If we were going to play the dom7#5 arpeggio on the V change instead of the whole tone scale, we might get something like this:

IIm7-Vdom7#5

(continued on next page)

My record date in NYC, Jan. 2008 - (standing from the left) Dave Kikoski, keys, Randy Brecker, tpt, Chuggy Carter, perc, Graham Hawthorne, drums, and Victor Bailey, bass. (sitting) engineer Joe Berger and me.

Or this one, with two bars on each chord change:

IIm7-Vdom7#5 (2 bars each)

129

If we choose to make the V change a dom7b5, we can certainly do that as well. We can go with the two-bar harmonic regions again:

IIm7-Vdom7b5 (2 bars each)

Or one bar - or two beats - apiece:

IIm7-Vdom7b5 (1 bar or 2 beats each)

There really are TONS of different alterations we can use on that Vdom7 change, either coming from the regular IIm7 or the IIm7b5. I'm sure you will agree that we should just play through as many possible variations as we can think of!

We can go from IIm7 to Vdom13b9, which can create a pattern of chromatically descending major triads if we play the entire progression down in whole steps:

IIm7-Vdom13b9

Or we can use the diminished (double extended) form on the V chord, which makes it a dom13b5b9 (played down chromatically this time):

IIm7-Vdom13b5b9

How about playing melodically down in 3rds from the 11 of the IIm7 (here a m7-9-11) and then using the tritone substitute major triad on the V to make a dom7b5b9? Or then again, we could outline the basic chords in an upward pattern for 2 beats each and play that one in whole steps:

(See following page)

IIm7-Vdom7b5b9

We can go from the IIm7 to a Vdom7#5b9 - which outlines the minor triad a half step above the Vdom7 (that minor triad would be the root chord of the melodic minor scale from which we get the altered 7th scale to play here). Notice the Eb minor triad against the D7#5b9 in the first sequence:

IIm7-Vdom7#5b9

Or we can get really jazzy and adventurous and make a 13#9 on the V chord... and throw in a b5 for good measure!

And there is always the dom7#5#9 possibility on the V - here is that maj7b5 chord form again, played over the bass note a major 3rd below to turn its degrees into 3-#5-b7-#9!

IIm7-Vdom7#5#9

Let's move now to the m7b5 option for our II chords. Of course there are a great number of variations available here as well. We can start with a few going to the straight 5dom7 chord, first chromatically:

Chromatic IIm7b5 - Vdom7

And these babies also sound very nice going down in whole steps, don't you agree?
(We'll shift down a half step after 6 bars to cover all the keys!)

IIm7b5 - Vdom7 (whole steps)

SECTION IV ● ● ● ● ● ● ● ● ● ● ● ● ● ● ● ● ● ● ●

You are probably aware that the m7b5 is also known as the *half-diminished 7th* chord. This is be-cause there is only a one note difference - the b7 instead of the major 6th - between any m7b5 chord and an actual diminished 7th chord. But if we drop that b7 a half step it will sound like it is resolving to the 3rd of the dom7b9 chord that that diminished 7th chord also is!

IIm7b5 - Vdom7b9

139

All the harmonically hippest and most colorful alterations really stand out and shine in the minor II-V. Particularly the ones from the altered scale! We'll stretch these out for a bar apiece - again, so we can fully appreciate their tonal colors.

a)

IIm7b5 - Vdom7#5#9

(continued on next page)

b)

c)

IIm7b5-Vdom7#5#9

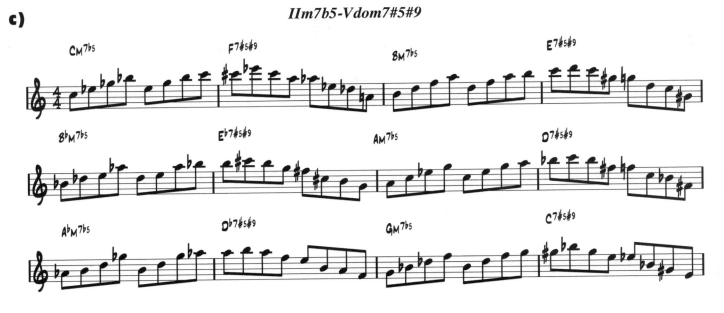

(continued on next page)

Remember those 2 major triads from the altered scale that contain either the #5#9 or the b5b9?
We can accent both of them if we like:

IIm7b5 - Vdom7b5b9 or #5#9 (two triads)

Or we can make the II a *m9b5* and on the V, play the bII minor triad (#5b9 against the 5) going to an augmented triad, OR a b5b9 *major* triad going to a bII minor!

IIm7b5 - Vdom7 (altered)

By the way... did we mention that just taking our basic IIm7b5 chord and moving it *up a minor third* creates a Vdom7#5b9 - with the 1-b3-b5-b7 becoming the b7-b9-3-#5 over the V in the bass? So I think it would be a good thing for us to practice those arpeggios going up in minor thirds from all their possible starting notes!

IIm7b5 - Vdom7#5b9

We can also shift between those two arpeggios within one octave:

IIm7b5 - Vdom7#5b9

We can do the same thing with the maj7b5 chord form that we so know and love as a Vdom7#5#9.
That same arpeggio a minor third below can substitute for the IIm7b5, containing the b5-b7-1 and 4
- so it is kind of a m7b5(sus). In any case, we can move those maj7b5 arpeggios up in minor 3rds to
get the same minor II-V effect:

IIm7b5(sus) - Vdom7#5#9 (maj7b5's up in minor thirds)

And we can do the same upward minor 3rd motion again with the maj7#5 - which over the II becomes a *m9b5(sus)* while the V chord becomes a #5#9 without the 7th.

IIm9b5(sus) - Vdom7#5#9 (maj7#5's in minor thirds)

Another tasty tidbit we can throw in is to use the quartal triads containing the altered 7th scale degrees - the b5, #5 ,b9, and #9 - against the V chord. Sometimes we might want to play them in conjunction with the 3 and b7 of the dom7 chord to add a little anchor to our harmonic excursions!

(See following page)

IIm7b5 - Vdom7alt (w/quartal triads)

Or we can just play *only* those altered tones over the V chord and stretch that harmony out! These might sound a little more inside if we have a chordal instrument playing an alt7th behind us.

IIm7b5 - Vdom7alt (w/quartal triads)

There is one more fun little thing we can do with the II-V, and that is to use substitute changes on the V chord. Instead of one full bar of IIm7, we can play IIm7-Vdom7 for the first bar and then add a bit of color with the II-V changes for the *tritone substitute of the V chord* on the second bar. This gives us two beats each of IIm7-Vdom7 and *bVIm7-bIIdom7!* The bIIdom7 is of course a dom7b5b9 against the original V (or a #5b9 in its upper part). (See following page.)

IIm7 - Vdom7 - bVIm7 - bIIdom7

Part 5 The Dominance of Dominants!

You gotta love those dominant 7th chords! Their funky, bluesy quality takes us right along with them when we play their arpeggios! We should definitely practice them every which way! Chromatically, for instance, up and down:

Dom7th chords (1 bar - down chromatically)

Dom7th chords (2 beats - down chromatically)

Dom7th chords (1 bar - up chromatically)

Dom7th chords (2 beats - up chromatically)

And up and down in whole steps is good too. We'll do groups of six bars here just so we can be sure to cover all the keys:

Dom7th chords (1 bar - down in whole steps)

Dom7th chords (1 bar - up in whole steps)

And why not do two beats apiece in whole steps as well?

Dom7th chords (2 beats - up and down in whole steps)

Playing our dominant 7th chords in minor 3rds takes us into 100% pure diminished scale territory. So it would follow that if we so choose, we could play these patterns against *any* of the four dom7th chords in each four-chord sequence! (Note: every one of these is different, so I recommend transposing them into the other two diminished scales.)

Dom7th chords (up and down in minor 3rds)

I don't think it is really necessary to write out a page of dom7th chords in major 3rds here, although one will indeed encounter that chord sequence from time to time. If you feel like practicing them that way, you are more than welcome to do so! But dom7th chords in the circle of 4ths are another story! There is no doubt that we can benefit from playing plenty of them!

Dom7th chords (2 beats - circle of 4ths)

Dom7th chords (2 beats - circle of 4ths)

Dom7th chords (2 beats - circle of 4ths)

Dom7b5 chords are fun through the circle of 4ths as well. Notice how the second group of six chords are inversions of the first six! And also how descending chromatically produces an inversion of the same chords going up in 4ths!

Dom7b5 chords (2 beats - circle of 4ths)

And let's not forget those dom7#5's!

Dom7#5 chords (2 beats - circle of 4ths)

And there is plenty of stuff we can do with the dom7b9 (also dim7) arpeggio through the circle of 4ths. Since the arpeggio is so incredibly symmetrical, playing it down chromatically, up in whole steps - or even down in major 3rds – gives us inversions of the same chords going up in 4ths!

Dom7b9 chords (2 beats - circle of 4ths)

Dom7b9 chords (2 beats - circle of 4ths)

When we play the dom7#5#9 - or its tritone substitute, the dom9#11(13) - through the circle of 4ths, the *upper extension triads* go through the circle as well:

Dom7#5#9/Dom9#11(13) chords (1 bar - circle of 4ths)

The same goes for the dom7b5b9 with its upper structure triad a tritone removed from the bass note.

Dom7b5b9 chords (circle of 4ths)

And by the way.... would anyone care for a lovely bunch of dom13b9's?

(See following page)

Dom13b9 chords (circle of 4ths)

Or how about some dom13#9's? Notice here again - since we are playing only the chord degrees 3-b7-#9-13 - that the notes in the second six chords are inversions of the first six!

Dom13#9 chords (circle of 4ths)

And of course we can always go back to the good old plain dom7(9-13) chord again, the maj7b5 form made up of degrees b7-9-3-13. Playing that one down chromatically against the circle of 4ths bass notes creates a pattern of dom9(13) - dom7#5#9 chords!

Dom9(13) - dom7#5#9 chords (circle of 4ths)

And we can't forget to do some variations on V-I progressions!

Vdom7(13) - Imaj (6/9 or 2)

Vdom7(alt) - Imin (6/9 or major7)

Vdom7b9 or #5b9 - I major or minor

We can choose to resolve our V chord to a quartal triad (1-2-5) that could be either major or minor!

Vdom7(various alterations) - 1-2-5 quartal triad

Part 6 • Turnaround Corner!

And it's always a good thing to have plenty of those turnarounds in our musical vocabulary. Why don't we play the first 8 bars of rhythm changes in all 12 keys? (Needless to say, any one of these two-bar bits can *also* be run through all the keys!)

Turnarounds (rhythm changes - first 8 bars - 12 keys)

Turnarounds (rhythm changes - first 8 bars - 12 keys)

Turnarounds (rhythm changes - first 8 bars in B and a chorus in Bb!)

PART 7 Other Combinations of Stuff

I'm not finished with you yet! There is a lot of other stuff we can do. There are things with major 7th chords:

Maj7th chords up and down in minor 3rds

Maj7 - maj7b5 - maj7#5

And think of all the possible bass notes that could go under these:

Maj7b5 chords (circle of 4ths)

Maj7#5 chords (circle of 4ths)

Of course, those maj7#5's could be minor 9th chords with a major 7th as well:

Min9(maj7) chords down in whole steps

Care for something pretty and melodic? We can do Imaj7 going to IVm6 and take that sequence up in minor 3rds (of course, that IVm6 can also be the Vdom7(9) of the following maj7 chord!):

Imaj7 - IVm6 chords (up in minor 3rds)

Or we can go totally outside with a diminished(double extended) form—and play sequences in a variety of different combinations—taking it down a 4th and up a minor 3rd, up a minor 3rd and down a half step, etc... I'll leave it to you to figure out what the harmony could be here.

Diminished (double extended) combinations

SECTION IV ● ● ● ● ● ● ● ● ● ● ● ● ● ● ● ● ● ● ●

There are a bunch of things we can do with quartal triads as well. These babies can always be used modally:

Quartal triads - modal

Or we can play them in various chromatic combinations. But each individual triad fits into so many keys that they can be analyzed in a lot of different ways! See how many different chords you can fit these bits into, using the first two lines as an example.

Quartal triads - chromatic and minor 3rd combinations

Using the quartal triads that contain a tritone in conjunction with the straight 4th can create some nice phrygian and bluesy effects:

Quartal triads - perfect 4th and tritone combinations

And finally, here is one of my own personal favorites: playing combinations of the quartal triads... but using the pentatonic scale as the lead melody note!

F minor pentatonic w/quartal triads

There are surely as many possible combinations of harmony and melody as there are leaves on the trees or ideas in the imagination! The only boundaries are the ones we choose to create! I sincerely hope that the materials in this book will enlighten and inspire some of the great jazz artists of tomorrow.

But let us not forget: despite all the intellectual analysis and physical labor (practicing!) that we must do to learn our craft, music - *as an art* - is ultimately about the *feeling* we put into it, the *sharing* with our audience - and the *expression* of what is in our soul.

All the best,

Chord/Scale Index

(All scales are from the root of the chord unless otherwise noted)

CHORD	SCALE
maj7, maj9, maj6/9, maj7/6	major or lydian
maj7b5	lydian
maj7#5	melodic minor scale a minor third below (3rd mode - also known as lydian#5)
minor7	dorian, phrygian or natural minor
m9, m9/11	dorian or natural minor
m7(sus)	dorian, phrygian, or natural minor
m6, m13, m6/9	dorian or whole-step diminished
m7b5	locrian or melodic minor a minor third above (6th mode - also known as locrian ♮2)
m7#5	phrygian, locrian or locrian ♮2
m9b5	locrian ♮2
m(maj7), m9(maj7)	melodic minor
dom7, dom7(9), dom7(13)	mixolydian or lydian dominant (melodic minor a fifth above)
dom7(sus), dom(9-11), dom(9-11-13)	mixolydian
dom7(9-#11), dom(9-#11-13)	lydian dominant

(continued on next page)

CHORD	SCALE
dom7b5	whole tone, lydian dominant, half-step diminished or altered (melodic minor a half step above)
dom7#5	C whole tone or altered
dom9b5, 9#5	whole tone
dom7b9, 7#9	half-step diminished or (if there is no 5th in the altered chord)
dom13b9, 13#9, 13b5b9	half-step diminished
dom7b5b9, b5#9	half-step diminished or altered
dom7#5b9, #5#9	altered
dim7, dim(extended) or (double extended)	whole-step diminished
anything else	the chromatic scale!!

The finest in Jazz & Latin publications

See www.shermusic.com for more information, including a complete list of tunes in all our fake books.
To order, call (800) 444-7437 or fax (707) 763-2038

The New Real Book Series

The Standards Real Book (C, Bb or Eb)

Alice In Wonderland
All Of You
Alone Together
At Last
Baltimore Oriole
A Beautiful Friendship
Bess, You Is My Woman
But Not For Me
Close Enough For Love
Crazy He Calls Me
Dancing In The Dark
Days Of Wine And Roses
Dreamsville
Easy To Love
Embraceable You

Falling In Love With Love
From This Moment On
Give Me The Simple Life
Have You Met Miss Jones?
Hey There
I Can't Get Started
I Concentrate On You
I Cover The Waterfront
I Love You
I Loves You Porgy
I Only Have Eyes For You
I Wish I Knew
I'm A Fool To Want You
Indian Summer
It Ain't Necessarily So

It Never Entered My Mind
It's You Or No One
Just One Of Those Things
Love For Sale
Love Walked In
Lover, Come Back To Me
The Man I Love
Mr. Lucky
My Funny Valentine
My Heart Stood Still
My Man's Gone Now
Old Folks
On A Clear Day
Our Love Is Here To Stay
Secret Love

September In The Rain
Serenade In Blue
Shiny Stockings
Since I Fell For You
So In Love
So Nice (Summer Samba)
Some Other Time
Stormy Weather
The Summer Knows
Summer Night
Summertime
Teach Me Tonight
That Sunday, That Summer
Then I'll Be Tired Of You
There's No You

A Time For Love
Time On My Hands
'Tis Autumn
Where Or When
Who Cares?
With A Song In My Heart
You Go To My Head
Ain't No Sunshine
'Round Midnight
The Girl From Ipanema
Bluesette
And Hundreds More!

The New Real Book - Volume 1 (C, Bb or Eb)

Angel Eyes
Anthropology
Autumn Leaves
Beautiful Love
Bernie's Tune
Blue Bossa
Blue Daniel
But Beautiful
Chain Of Fools
Chelsea Bridge
Compared To What
Darn That Dream
Desafinado
Early Autumn
Eighty One

E.S.P.
Everything Happens To Me
Fall
Feel Like Makin' Love
Footprints
Four
Four On Six
Gee Baby Ain't I Good
To You
Gone With The Wind
Here's That Rainy Day
I Love Lucy
I Mean You
I Should Care
I Thought About You

If I Were A Bell
Imagination
The Island
Jersey Bounce
Joshua
Lady Bird
Like Someone In Love
Line For Lyons
Little Sunflower
Lush Life
Mercy, Mercy, Mercy
The Midnight Sun
Monk's Mood
Moonlight In Vermont
My Shining Hour

Nature Boy
Nefertiti
Nothing Personal
Oleo
Once I Loved
Out Of This World
Pent Up House
Polkadots And Moon-
beams
Portrait Of Tracy
Put It Where You Want It
Robbin's Nest
Ruby, My Dear
Satin Doll
Search For Peace

Shaker Song
Skylark
A Sleepin' Bee
Solar
Speak No Evil
St. Thomas
Street Life
Tenderly
These Foolish Things
This Masquerade
Three Views Of A Secret
Waltz For Debby
Willow Weep For Me
And Many More!

The New Real Book - Volume 2 (C, Bb or Eb)

Afro-Centric
After You've Gone
Along Came Betty
Bessie's Blues
Black Coffee
Blues For Alice
Body And Soul
Bolivia
The Boy Next Door
Bye Bye Blackbird
Cherokee
A Child Is Born
Cold Duck Time
Day By Day

Django
Equinox
Exactly Like You
Falling Grace
Five Hundred Miles High
Freedom Jazz Dance
Giant Steps
Got A Match?
Harlem Nocturne
Hi-Fly
Honeysuckle Rose
I Hadn't Anyone 'Til You
I'll Be Around
I'll Get By

Ill Wind
I'm Glad There Is You
Impressions
In Your Own Sweet Way
It's The Talk Of The Town
Jordu
Killer Joe
Lullaby Of The Leaves
Manha De Carneval
The Masquerade Is Over
Memories Of You
Moment's Notice
Mood Indigo
My Ship

Naima
Nica's Dream
Once In A While
Perdido
Rosetta
Sea Journey
Senor Blues
September Song
Seven Steps To Heaven
Silver's Serenade
So Many Stars
Some Other Blues
Song For My Father
Sophisticated Lady

Spain
Stablemates
Stardust
Sweet And Lovely
That's All
There Is No Greater Love
'Til There Was You
Time Remembered
Turn Out The Stars
Unforgettable
While We're Young
Whisper Not
Will You Still Be Mine?
You're Everything
And Many More!

The New Real Book - Volume 3 (C, Bb, Eb or Bass clef)

Actual Proof
Ain't That Peculiar
Almost Like Being In Love
Another Star
Autumn Serenade
Bird Of Beauty
Black Nile
Blue Moon
Butterfly
Caravan
Ceora
Close Your Eyes
Creepin'
Day Dream

Dolphin Dance
Don't Be That Way
Don't Blame Me
Emily
Everything I Have Is Yours
For All We Know
Freedomland
The Gentle Rain
Get Ready
A Ghost Of A Chance
Heat Wave
How Sweet It Is
I Fall In Love Too Easily
I Got It Bad

I Hear A Rhapsody
If You Could See Me Now
In A Mellow Tone
In A Sentimental Mood
Inner Urge
Invitation
The Jitterbug Waltz
Just Friends
Just You, Just Me
Knock On Wood
The Lamp Is Low
Laura
Let's Stay Together
Lonely Woman

Maiden Voyage
Moon And Sand
Moonglow
My Girl
On Green Dolphin Street
Over The Rainbow
Prelude To A Kiss
Respect
Ruby
The Second Time Around
Serenata
The Shadow Of Your Smile
So Near, So Far
Solitude

Speak Like A Child
Spring Is Here
Stairway To The Stars
Star Eyes
Stars Fell On Alabama
Stompin' At The Savoy
Sweet Lorraine
Taking A Chance On Love
This Is New
Too High
(Used To Be A) Cha Cha
When Lights Are Low
You Must Believe In Spring
And Many More!

The New Real Book Play-Along CDs (For Volume 1)

CD #1 - Jazz Classics - Lady Bird, Bouncin' With Bud, Up Jumped Spring, Monk's Mood, Doors, Very Early, Eighty One, Voyage **& More!**
CD #2 - Choice Standards - Beautiful Love, Darn That Dream, Moonlight In Vermont, Trieste, My Shining Hour, I Should Care **& More!**
CD #3 - Pop-Fusion - Morning Dance, Nothing Personal, La Samba, Hideaway, This Masquerade, Three Views Of A Secret, Rio **& More!**
World-Class Rhythm Sections, featuring Mark Levine, Larry Dunlap, Sky Evergreen, Bob Magnusson, Keith Jones, Vince Lateano & Tom Hayashi

Recent Sher Music Publications

Afro-Caribbean Grooves for Drumset

By **Jean-Philippe Fanfant,** drummer with Andy narell's band, Sakesho.

Covers grooves from 10 Caribbean nations, arranged for drumset. **CD includes both audio and video files.** $25.

Endorsed by Peter Erskine, Horacio Hernandez, etc.

The Real Easy Book Vol. 3
A SHORT HISTORY OF JAZZ

Published by Sher Music Co. in conjunction with the Stanford Jazz Workshop. Over 200 pages. $25.

History text and tunes from all eras and styles of jazz. Perfect for classroom use. Available in C, Bb, Eb and Bass Clef versions.

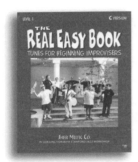

The Real Easy Book Vol. 1
TUNES FOR BEGINNING IMPROVISERS

Published by Sher Music Co. in conjunction with the Stanford Jazz Workshop. $19 list price.

The easiest tunes from Horace Silver, Eddie Harris, Freddie Hubbard, Red Garland, Sonny Rollins, Cedar Walton, Wes Montgomery Cannonball Adderly, etc. Get yourself or your beginning jazz combo sounding good right away with the first fake book ever designed for the beginning improviser.
Available in C, Bb, Eb and Bass Clef.

The Real Easy Book Vol. 2
TUNES FOR INTERMEDIATE IMPROVISERS

Published by Sher Music Co. in conjunction with the Stanford Jazz Workshop. Over 240 pages. $29.

The best intermediate-level tunes by: Charlie Parker, John Coltrane, Miles Davis, John Scofield, Sonny Rollins, Horace Silver, Wes Montgomery, Freddie Hubbard, Cal Tjader, Cannonball Adderly, and more! Both volumes feature instructional material tailored for each tune. Perfect for jazz combos! Available in C, Bb, Eb and Bass Clef.

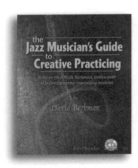

The Jazz Musicians Guide To Creative Practicing

By **David Berkman**

Finally a book to help musicians use their practice time wisely! Covers tune analysis, breaking hard tunes into easy components, how to swing better, tricks to playing fast bebop lines, and much more! 150+pages, plus CD. $29 list.

"Fun to read and bursting with things to do and ponder." – Bob Mintzer

The Serious Jazz Practice Book By Barry Finnerty

Includes CD - $30 list price. A unique and comprehensive plan for mastering the basic building blocks of the jazz language. It takes the most widely-used scales and chords and gives you step-by-step exercises that dissect them into hundreds of cool, useable patterns.

"The book I've been waiting for!" – Randy Brecker.

"The best book of intervallic studies I've ever seen." – Mark Levine

The All Jazz Real Book

Over 540 pages of tunes as recorded by: Miles, Trane, Bill Evans, Cannonball, Scofield, Brecker, Yellowjackets, Bird, Mulgrew Miller, Kenny Werner, MJQ, McCoy Tyner, Kurt Elling, Brad Mehldau, Don Grolnick, Kenny Garrett, Patitucci, Jerry Bergonzi, Stanley Clarke, Tom Harrell, Herbie Hancock, Horace Silver, Stan Getz, Sonny Rollins, and MORE!

Includes a free CD of many of the melodies (featuring Bob Sheppard & Friends.). $44 list price. Available in C, Bb, Eb

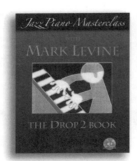

Jazz Piano Masterclass With Mark Levine
"THE DROP 2 BOOK"

The long-awaited book from the author of "The Jazz Piano Book!" A complete study on how to use "drop 2" chord voicings to create jazz piano magic! 68 pages, plus CD of Mark demonstrating each exercise. $19 list.

"Will make you sound like a real jazz piano player in no time." – Jamey Aebersold

Metaphors For The Musician
By **Randy Halberstadt**

This practical and enlightening book will help any jazz player or vocalist look at music with "new eyes." Designed for any level of player, on any instrument, "Metaphors For The Musician" provides numerous exercises throughout to help the reader turn these concepts into musical reality.

Guaranteed to help you improve your musicianship. 330 pages - $29 list price. Satisfaction guaranteed!

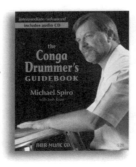

The Conga Drummer's Guidebook By Michael Spiro

Includes CD - $28 list price. The only method book specifically designed for the intermediate to advanced conga drummer. It goes behind the superficial licks and explains how to approach any Afro-Latin rhythm with the right feel, so you can create a groove like the pros!.

"This book is awesome. Michael is completely knowledgable about his subject." – Dave Garibaldi

"A breakthrough book for all students of the conga drum." – Karl Perazzo

Latin Music Books & CDs

The Latin Real Book (C, Bb or Eb)

The only professional-level Latin fake book ever published! Over 570 pages. Includes detailed transcriptions of tunes, exactly as recorded by:

Ray Barretto	Irakere	Andy Narell	Ft. Apache Band	Djavan
Eddie Palmieri	Celia Cruz	Mario Bauza	Dave Valentin	Tom Jobim
Fania All-Stars	Arsenio Rodriguez	Dizzy Gilllespie	Paquito D'Rivera	Toninho Horta
Tito Puente	Tito Rodriguez	Mongo Santamaria	Clare Fischer	Joao Bosco
Ruben Blades	Orquesta Aragon	Manny Oquendo & Libre	Chick Corea	Milton Nascimento
Los Van Van	Beny Moré	Puerto Rico All-Stars	Sergio Mendes	Leila Pinheiro
NG La Banda	Cal Tjader	Issac Delgaldo	Ivan Lins	Gal Costa
				And Many More!

Muy Caliente!
Afro-Cuban Play-Along CD and Book
Rebeca Mauleón - Keyboard
Oscar Stagnaro - Bass
Orestes Vilató - Timbales
Carlos Caro - Bongos
Edgardo Cambon - Congas
Over 70 min. of smokin' Latin grooves! Stereo separation so you can eliminate the bass or piano. Play-along with a rhythm section featuring some of the top Afro-Cuban musicians in the world!

The Latin Real Book Sampler CD

12 of the greatest Latin Real Book tunes as played by the original artists: Tito Puente, Ray Barretto, Andy Narell, Puerto Rico Allstars, Bacacoto, etc.
$16 list price. Available in U.S.A. only.

101 Montunos
by Rebeca Mauleón

The only comprehensive study of Latin piano playing ever published.

- Bi-lingual text (English/Spanish)
- 2 CDs of the author demonstrating each montuno
- Covers over 100 years of Afro-Cuban styles, including the danzón, guaracha, mambo, merengue and songo—from Peruchin to Eddie Palmieri.

The True Cuban Bass
By Carlos Del Puerto, (bassist with Irakere) and **Silvio Vergara**, $22.

For acoustic or electric bass; English and Spanish text; Includes CDs of either historic Cuban recordings or Carlos playing each exercise; Many transcriptions of complete bass parts for tunes in different Cuban styles – the roots of Salsa.

The Brazilian Guitar Book
by Nelson Faria, one of Brazil's best new guitarists.

- Over 140 pages of comping patterns, transcriptions and chord melodies for samba, bossa, baião, etc.
- Complete chord voicings written out for each example.
- Comes with a CD of Nelson playing each example.
- The most complete Brazilian guitar method ever published! $28 list price.

Joe Diorio – "Nelson Faria's book is a welcome addition to the guitar literature. I'm sure those who work with this volume wiiill benefit greatly"

The Salsa Guide Book
By Rebeca Mauleón

The only complete method book on salsa ever published! 260 pages. $25

Carlos Santana – "A true treasure of knowledge and information about Afro-Cuban music."
Mark Levine, author of The Jazz Piano Book. – "This is the book on salsa."
Sonny Bravo, pianist with Tito Puente – "This will be the salsa 'bible' for years to come."
Oscar Hernández, pianist with Rubén Blades – "An excellent and much needed resource."

The Latin Bass Book
A PRACTICAL GUIDE
By Oscar Stagnaro

The only comprehensive book ever published on how to play bass in authentic Afro-Cuban, Brazilian, Caribbean, Latin Jazz & South American styles. $34 list price

Over 250 pages of transcriptions of Oscar Stagnaro playing each exercise. Learn from the best!

Includes: 3 Play-Along CDs to accompany each exercise, featuring world-class rhythm sections.

Inside The Brazilian Rhythm Section
By Nelson Faria and Cliff Korman

This is the first book/CD package ever published that provides an opportunity for bassists, guitarists, pianists and drummers to interact and play-along with a master Brazilian rhythm section. Perfect for practicing both accompanying and soloing.

$28 list price for book and 2 CDs - including the charts for the CD tracks and sample parts for each instrument, transcribed from the recording. Satisfaction guaranteed!

More Jazz Publications

The Digital Real Book

On the web

Over 850 downloadable tunes from all the Sher Music Co. fakebooks.

See www.shermusic.com for details.

Walking Bassics: The Fundamentals of Jazz Bass Playing

By swinging NY bassist Ed Fuqua

Includes transcriptions of every bass note on **accompanying CD** and step-by-step method for constructing solid walking bass lines. $22.

Endorsed by Eddie Gomez, Jimmy Haslip, John Goldsby, etc.

The Jazz Theory Book

By Mark Levine, the most comprehensive Jazz Theory book ever published! $38 list price.

- Over 500 pages of text and over 750 musical examples.
- Written in the language of the working jazz musician, this book is easy to read and user-friendly. At the same time, it is the most comprehensive study of jazz harmony and theory ever published.
- Mark Levine has worked with Bobby Hutcherson, Cal Tjader, Joe Henderson, Woody Shaw, and many other jazz greats.

The European Real Book

An amazing collection of some of the greatest jazz compositions ever recorded! Available in C, Bb and Eb. $40

- Over 100 of Europe's best jazz writers.
- 100% accurate, composer-approved charts.
- 400 pages of fresh, exciting sounds from virtually every country in Europe.
- Sher Music's superior legibility and signature calligraphy makes reading the music easy.

Listen to FREE MP3 FILES of many of the songs at **www.shermusic.com!**

The Jazz Piano Book

By Mark Levine, Concord recording artist and pianist with Cal Tjader. For beginning to advanced pianists. The only truly comprehensive method ever published! Over 300 pages. $32

Richie Beirach –"The best new method book available."
Hal Galper – "This is a must!"
Jamey Aebersold – "This is an invaluable resource for any pianist."
James Williams – "One of the most complete anthologies on jazz piano."

Also available in Spanish! ¡El Libro del Jazz Piano!

Concepts For Bass Soloing

By Chuck Sher and Marc Johnson, (bassist with Bill Evans, etc.) The only book ever published that is specifically designed to improve your soloing! $26

- Includes two CDs of Marc Johnson soloing on each exercise
- Transcriptions of bass solos by: Eddie Gomez, John Patitucci, Scott LaFaro, Jimmy Haslip, etc.

"It's a pleasure to encounter a Bass Method so well conceived and executed." – **Steve Swallow**

The Yellowjackets Songbook

Complete package contains six separate spiral-bound books, one each for:
- Piano/partial score • C melody lead sheet
- Synthesizer/miscellaneous parts
- Bb & Eb Horn melody part • Bass • Drums

Contains 20 great tunes from their entire career. Charts exactly as recorded – approved by the Yellowjackets. World famous Sher Music Co. accuracy and legibility. Over 400 pages, $38 list price.

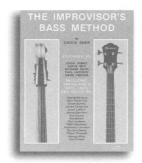

The Improvisor's Bass Method

By Chuck Sher. A complete method for electric or acoustic bass, plus transcribed solos and bass lines by Mingus, Jaco, Ron Carter, Scott LaFaro, Paul Jackson, Ray Brown, and more! Over 200 pages. $16

International Society of Bassists – "Undoubtedly the finest book of its kind."
Eddie Gomez – "Informative, readily comprehensible and highly imaginative"

The World's Greatest Fake Book

Jazz & Fusion Tunes by: **Coltrane, Mingus, Jaco, Chick Corea, Bird, Herbie Hancock, Bill Evans, McCoy, Beirach, Ornette, Wayne Shorter, Zawinul, AND MANY MORE!** $32

Chick Corea – "Great for any students of jazz.'
Dave Liebman – "The fake book of the 80's."
George Cables – "The most carefully conceived fake book I've ever seen."

The Jazz Solos of Chick Corea

Over 150 pages of Chick's greatest solos; "Spain", "Litha", "Windows", "Sicily", etc. for all instrumentalists, single line transcriptions, not full piano score. $18

Chick Corea – "I don't know anyone I would trust more to correctly transcribe my improvisations."